ÜBERDENTELLERRANDKOCHEN

DAS KOCHBUCH
THE COOKBOOK

REZEPTE FÜR EIN BESSERES WIR

RECIPES FOR A BETTER US

ÜBERDENTELLERRANDKOCHEN

VORWORT

Dieses Buch ist mehr als ein gewöhnliches Rezeptbuch.
Es ist mehr als ein buntes Potpourri aus internationalen Originalrezepten.
Es ist mehr als eine Sammlung von Erfahrungen der Menschen, die in Deutschland ein Zuhause suchen.
Es ist mehr als die Geschichte von Leuten, die ihre Mitmenschen willkommen heißen.
Es ist mehr als die Summe von Begegnungen zwischen Personen unterschiedlicher Kulturen.
Es ist die Dokumentation einer Gesellschaft, die zusammenwächst.

Entstanden aus einem Aufruf, der Menschen verschiedener Kulturen zum Kochen zusammenführte, weitergetragen durch all jene, die das Thema Asyl aus einem anderen Blickwinkel betrachten möchten und ermöglicht durch Dich.

Die Erfahrungen aus über 30 Kochbegegnungen, die Rezepte aus aller Welt und die ganz persönlichen Geschichten der Flüchtlinge, haben wir in diesem Buch zusammengefasst, um noch viele andere zu inspirieren aufeinander zuzugehen.

Koch' auch Du über den Tellerrand und trage damit bei zu einem besseren WIR.

Mehr über das Projekt und darüber, wie dieses Buch entstanden ist, findest Du auf den Seiten 11 und 210.

MENSCHEN DURCH KOCHEN ZUSAMMENZUBRINGEN WAR DIE BESTE ERFAHRUNG, DIE ICH JE GEMACHT HABE.

Amani

BRINGING PEOPLE TOGETHER BY COOKING
IS THE BEST EXPERIENCE I HAVE EVER HAD.

Amani

PREFACE

This book is more than an ordinary recipe book.
It is more than a potpourri of international and original recipes.
It is more than the experiences of people who are looking for a home in Germany.
It is more than the story of those people who welcome their fellow human beings.
It is more than a collection of encounters between people from different cultures.
It is the documentary of a society that is growing together.

It is the result of a call that connected people from different cultures to cook together, carried out by those who want to see the theme of asylum from a new angle and made possible by you.

In this book you will find the experiences from more than 30 cooking encounters. We hope that these recipes from around the world and the personal stories of the refugees will inspire many more to approach one another.

You too can cook outside of the box and contribute to a united society!

You can find out more about the project and how this book was created on pages 11 and 210.

BEIM KOCHEN BRINGT MAN KULTUREN ZUSAMMEN.

Shaikh

UNSERE KÖCHINNEN UND KÖCHE

Die Köche und Köchinnen in diesem Buch sind als Flüchtlinge oder Asylsuchende nach Deutschland gekommen, um hier ein neues Zuhause zu finden. Sie bringen nicht nur außergewöhnliche Köstlichkeiten aus aller Welt, sondern auch viele spannende Geschichten über ihre Heimat und ihre Kultur mit, die sie in diesem Kochbuch mit uns teilen.

OUR COOKS

The cooks in this book came to Germany as refugees or asylum seekers in order to find a new home. In this cookbook, they share not only exceptional delicacies from around the world but also fascinating stories about their homeland and their culture.

COOKING IS ABOUT BRINGING CULTURES TOGETHER.

Shaikh

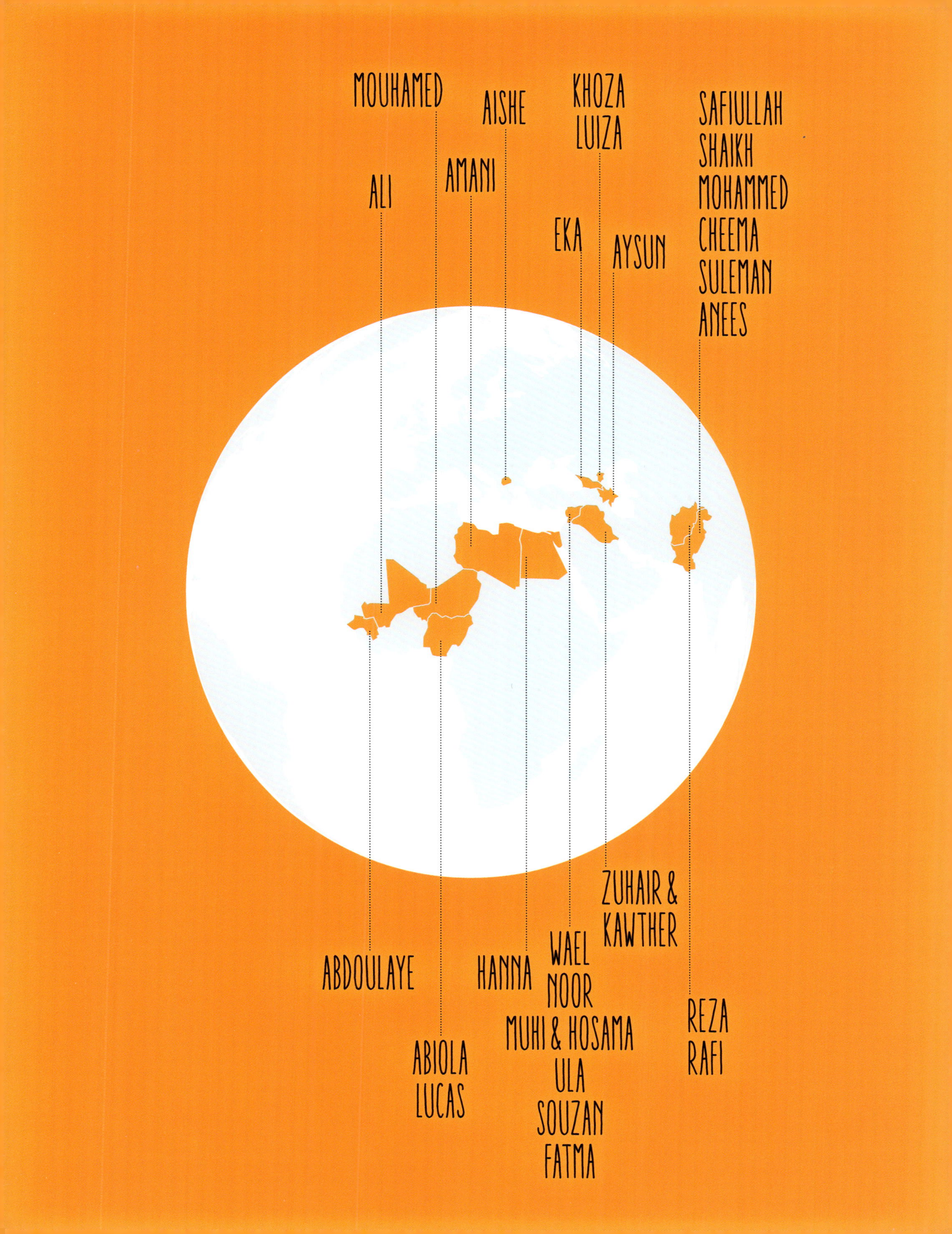
MOUHAMED
AISHE
KHOZA
LUIZA
SAFIULLAH
SHAIKH
MOHAMMED
CHEEMA
SULEMAN
ANEES
ALI
AMANI
EKA
AYSUN
ZUHAIR &
KAWTHER
ABDOULAYE
HANNA
WAEL
NOOR
MUHI & HOSAMA
ULA
SOUZAN
FATMA
REZA
RAFI
ABIOLA
LUCAS

INHALT · CONTENT

11 Wie dieses Kochbuch entstand
How this cookbook was created

12 Rezepte
Recipes

14 Wie das Kochbuch funktioniert
How the cookbook works

16 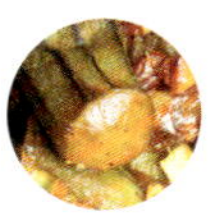
BHINDI
Cheema, Pakistan

22 
HAVIJ, GORME BADENJAN
Reza, Afghanistan

30 
CHICKEN CURRY
Anees, Pakistan

36 
TABOULEH
Ula, Syrien · Syria

42 
BIHARI, DHAL, PAKORAS
Shaikh, Pakistan

52 
MOJEDERA
Muhi & Hosama, Syrien · Syria

58 
CHASHUSHULI
Eka, Georgien · Georgia

64 
CHINGALSCH
Luiza, Tschetschenien · Chechnya

70 
KEEMA MATAR
Suleman, Pakistan

76 
HUMMUS
Fatma, Syrien · Syria

82 
DAMBOU
Mouhamed, Niger

88 
PLOW, DOLMA
Aysun, Aserbaidschan · Azerbaijan

96 
OOZIE
Wael, Syrien · Syria

102 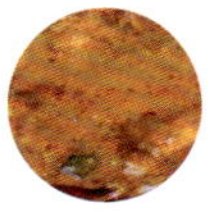 OGBONO SOUP
Abiola, Nigeria

108  BIRYANI
Safiullah, Pakistan

114  MA'ALOOBE, FASOOLYE BZEIT
Noor, Syrien · Syria

122  GALNASCH
Khoza, Tschetschenien · Chechnya

128  FALAFEL, COUSCOUS, IMBATEN
Amani, Libyen · Libya

138  ABERAX
Zuhair & Kawther, Irak · Iraq

144  KABULI PALAO
Rafi, Afghanistan

150  CROM MACHSCHIE, SHORBA ADS, BAMIA
Hanna, Ägypten · Egypt

160 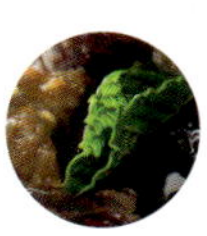 PALAT
Abdoulaye, Guinea

166  IZEE BI ISTEW
Lucas, Nigeria

172  SAMBUSAK
Souzan, Syrien · Syria

178  KHEER
Mohammed, Pakistan

184  CHOCOLATE ALMOND CAKE
Aishe, Mazedonien · Macedonia

190  DÉGUÊ
Ali, Mali

196 Deine eigenen Rezepte
Your own recipes

200 Zutatenverzeichnis
List of ingredients

208 Anhang
Appendix

DAS KOCHBUCH
THE COOKBOOK

WENN ICH KOCHE, TUE ICH ES AM LIEBSTEN FÜR ANDERE. DAS ESSEN SCHMECKT BESSER ZUSAMMEN MIT ANDEREN.

Rafi

I PREFER TO COOK FOR OTHERS. IT SIMPLY TASTES BETTER TOGETHER.

Rafi

WIE DIESES KOCHBUCH ENTSTAND...

In diesem Kochbuch findest Du außergewöhnliche Rezepte und interessante Geschichten von Menschen aus aller Welt, die jetzt in Deutschland eine neue Heimat suchen oder bereits gefunden haben. Gekocht und festgehalten wurden die Inhalte dieses Buches im Rahmen der deutschlandweiten *Mach Mit!*-Aktion von Über den Tellerrand kochen: Im Sommer 2014 riefen wir, das Team hinter diesem sozialen Projekt, Menschen in ganz Deutschland – ob Neuankömmlinge oder Beheimatete – zum gemeinsamen Kochen auf und vermittelten Interessierten den Kontakt zu Flüchtlingen vor Ort.

Mit diesem Aufruf wollten wir unsere eigenen positiven Erfahrungen teilen und zeigen, wie einfach es ist auf seine Mitmenschen zuzugehen und mit ihnen ein Miteinander zu gestalten – unabhängig von Kultur, Herkunft und Geschichte.

Die Reaktion auf diesen Aufruf war überwältigend, überall in Deutschland trafen sich Menschen aus aller Welt zum gemeinsamen Kochen. In Hamburg wurden nigerianische Speisen zubereitet, Düsseldorfer probierten afghanische Spezialitäten und in Bochum entstand ein ganzes Menü aus aserbaidschanischen Köstlichkeiten – es wurde gelacht, es wurden Geschichten geteilt und Freundschaften geschlossen.

Diese Erfahrungen hältst Du gerade in Deinen Händen. Ein Kochbuch voll von persönlichen Originalrezepten, exotischen Zutaten und den bewegenden Geschichten einer Gesellschaft, die zusammenwächst.

HOW THIS COOKBOOK WAS CREATED...

In this cookbook you will find extraordinary recipes and the fascinating stories of people from all over the world, people who would like to call Germany home or already do so. In the summer of 2014 we, the team behind this social project, launched our *Join in!*-campaign.

We called for people from all over Germany – whether newcomer or residents – to cook together. We connected refugees and residents who then cooked together and provided us with the recipes and stories you will find in this book. Through our call for action we were able to show how simple it can be to reach out to our fellow human beings and how easy it can be to create a feeling of togetherness – regardless of culture, origin and history.

The reaction to this call for action was overwhelming. The whole of Germany began meeting people from across the globe; they were meeting to cook together. Nigerian meals were rustled up in Hamburg, Düsseldorf tried its hand at Afghan specialties and Bochum produced an entire menu of Azerbaijani cuisine. Laughter was everywhere, stories were shared and friendships were created.

Now you are holding these experiences in your hands. A cookbook that is full of exotic ingredients, unique recipes and touching stories of a society that is growing together.

REZEPTE
RECIPES

WIE DAS KOCHBUCH FUNKTIONIERT…

Die Geschichten und Rezepte

Dieses Kochbuch gibt Dir die Möglichkeit neben außergewöhnlichen Rezepten aus aller Welt auch mehr über die Köche und Köchinnen selbst zu erfahren: Zu dem jeweiligen Gericht findest Du immer die Geschichte der Flüchtlinge oder Asylsuchenden, die dieses Rezept gekocht haben

Jeder Mensch bringt eigene Erfahrungen mit, jeder erzählt eine andere Geschichte und so ist jedes Kocherlebnis eine Reise in ein neues Land. Ob kurz oder lang, ob mit Foto oder ohne, ob ein Rezept oder gleich mehrere: Uns ist es wichtig, dass jede Geschichte so individuell bleibt, wie sie ist, von Autoren und Autorinnen aus ganz Deutschland verfasst, erzählt von Menschen aus der ganzen Welt.

Die Symbole

Um Dir das Kochen zu erleichtern, findest Du neben den Rezepten immer einige kleine Symbole:

35 Zubereitungszeit in Minuten

Schwierigkeitsgrad

Anzahl der Personen

vegane Variation

… und schon kann's losgehen!

Die Zutaten

Du weißt nicht, was Okras oder Ogbono sind? Du fragst dich, wo man Kochbananen und Tahina kaufen kann?

Kein Problem – besondere Zutaten sind mit einem gekennzeichnet. Zu diesen Zutaten findest Du eine genaue Erklärung im Zutatenverzeichnis ab Seite 202. Dort haben wir für Dich wichtige Informationen wie Herkunftsland, Beschreibung und Kaufmöglichkeit zusammengetragen.

Du hast Hunger auf noch mehr? Super – denn dann kannst Du Deine eigenen Kocherfahrungen und besonderen Rezepte am Ende des Buches ab Seite 196 selbst notieren!

Viel Spaß beim Kennenlernen, Erleben und über den Tellerrand Kochen!

HOW THE COOKBOOK WORKS...

The stories and recipes

This cookbook provides you not only with unique recipes from all over the world, but also with the opportunity to learn more about the cooks themselves. Alongside each recipe you will find the story of the refugee or asylum seeker who cooked and submitted the dish to us.

Every person has a different background, life and cooking experience – no two stories are alike. These recipes have been written by many authors from across Germany, the stories told by people from across the globe – but whether long or short, with a photo or without, whether one recipe or several, what is important to us is that each and every story remains as individual as it is.

The symbols

In order to simplify your cooking experience, you will find small symbols next to each recipe:

35 preparation time in minutes

level of difficulty

number of people

vegan variation

... and off you go!

The ingredients

So, you are not familiar with okra or ogbono? You wonder where to buy plantains or tahina? No problem – special ingredients are marked with a . You can find a detailed explanation of these ingredients in the list of ingredients on page 202. Here you will find information on the country of origin, description and place to purchase ingredients that appear in this book.

Hungry for more? Super! Jot down your own cooking experiences and special recipes at the end of this book at page 196.

Have fun cooking and reading through the Über den Tellerrand kochen experience!

CHEEMA

BHINDI

30

BHINDI

206

800 g Okraschoten
800 g okras

1 kg Zwiebeln, 1 Knoblauchknolle
1 kg onions, 1 garlic bulb

4 Tomaten
4 tomatoes

2 TL Garam Masala
2 tsp garam masala

204

½ TL Chilipulver
½ tsp chili powder

1 – 2 TL getrockneter Chili
1 – 2 tsp dried chili

2 Nelken
2 cloves

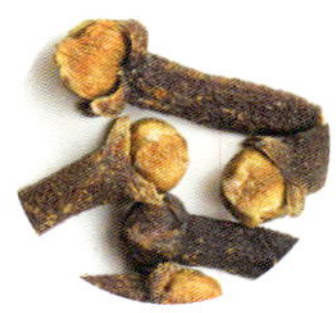

½ TL Kurkuma
½ tsp curcuma

1 TL Koriandersamen
1 tsp coriander seeds

¼ Zimtstange
¼ cinnamon stick

206

pakistanisches Brot oder Paratha
Pakistani bread or paratha

Salz, schwarzer Pfeffer, Pflanzenöl
salt, black pepper, vegetable oil

dieses Gericht ist vegan
this dish is vegan

MILDE GEMÜSEPFANNE MIT OKRA
VEGETABLE DISH WITH OKRA

- Zwiebeln in Ringe schneiden und Knoblauch fein hacken.
- Öl erhitzen und die Zwiebeln darin anbraten, bis sie glasig sind. Danach die gewürfelten Tomaten, Knoblauch, Salz, Garam Masala, Chilipulver, getrockneten Chili und Kurkuma hinzufügen.
- Ca. 10 min köcheln und reduzieren lassen.
- Koriandersamen, Nelken, Zimt und Pfeffer in beiden Händen zerreiben und ebenfalls in die Pfanne geben.
- Okraschoten zur reduzierten Masse hinzufügen und 10 min bei geschlossenem Deckel auf kleiner Flamme köcheln lassen, bis die Okraschoten leicht zerfallen.
- Mit pakistanischem Brot oder Paratha servieren.

- Slice the onions into rings and finely chop the garlic.
- Heat some oil and fry the onions. Then add the diced tomatoes, garlic, salt, garam masala, chili powder, dried chili, and curcuma.
- Simmer and allow to reduce for 10 min.
- Rub the coriander seeds, cloves, cinnamon, and pepper between your palms and then add to the pan.
- Add okras to the reduced onion mixture and simmer with the lid closed for another 10 min until the okras begin to disintegrate.
- Serve with Pakistani bread or paratha.

CHEEMA

Schon in der ersten Ausgabe des Über den Tellerrand kochen-Kochbuchs hat uns Cheema aus Pakistan mit seinem Gericht „Gurma" verzaubert. Auch dieses Mal wollte er sehr gerne dazu beitragen, dass eines seiner Lieblingsgerichte in die weite Welt getragen wird. Mittlerweile hat Cheema schon fleißig Deutsch gelernt und kann sich ganz gut verständigen. Vor allem ist er viel offener und selbstbewusster geworden, da er sich jetzt in seiner neuen Heimat und der Sprache etwas besser auskennt. Er lebt noch immer im Westen der Hauptstadt in einem Asylheim, möchte jedoch bald mit seinem besten Freund zusammen in eine richtige Wohnung ziehen. Cheema genießt seine freie Zeit am liebsten mit viel Ruhe und gutem Essen.

Lisa, Cheemas Kochpartnerin

Cheema is from Pakistan and already enchanted us with his dish "Gurma" in the first Über den Tellerand kochen cookbook. He was very keen to cook with us again and wanted to share one of his most favourite dishes with us – and the rest of the world!

Over the last few months, Cheema has been working hard to improve his German and can now understand and communicate the basics. We already met him last year and he has definitely become a lot more open and confident now that he knows his new home country and the language better. He lives in a home for asylum seekers, located to the west of Berlin. In the near future, Cheema hopes to move into his own flat with his best friend. What Cheema enjoys is relaxing in his free time with good food.

Lisa, Cheema's cooking partner

T
H

GORME BADENJAN HAVIJ

REZA

45 + 3 H

GORME BADENJAN

AFGHANISTAN

5 Auberginen
5 aubergines

3 Tassen Reis
3 cups of rice

1 Zwiebel
1 onion

Safran
saffron

4 Knoblauchzehen
4 cloves of garlic

1 Dose passierte Tomaten
1 can of sieved tomatoes

3 Kartoffeln
3 potatoes

1 EL Currypulver
1 tbsp curry powder

Salz, Pfeffer, Pflanzenöl
salt, pepper, vegetable oil

dieses Gericht ist vegan
this dish is vegan

Zubereitung vom Gorme Badenjan:

- Auberginen schälen und in 5 mm dicke Scheiben schneiden. Reichlich Öl in eine Pfanne geben und erhitzen.
  Die Auberginen nacheinander im Öl frittieren, bis sie sich bräunlich färben.
- Zwiebel und Knoblauch mit einer Reibe zu einer dickflüssigen Masse reiben. Die passierten Tomaten mit der Masse vermengen und mit Salz, Pfeffer und Curry würzen.
- Kartoffeln schälen und in 5 mm dicke Scheiben schneiden. Öl in einen großen Topf geben und den Boden mit den Kartoffelscheiben belegen. Dann abwechselnd Auberginen und Tomatensauce über die Kartoffeln schichten. Für etwa 20 min auf kleiner Flamme köcheln lassen.

Zubereitung vom Reis:

- Reis ca. 3 h in kaltem Wasser quellen lassen. Danach das Wasser abgießen und den Reis mit 6 Tassen frischem Wasser auf den Herd stellen.
- Ca. 15 min kochen, sodass er noch etwas Biss hat. Dann das Wasser abgießen, etwas Öl in eine tiefe Teflonpfanne schütten und den Reis dazugeben. Den Herd auf eine niedrige Stufe stellen. Den Deckel der Pfanne in ein Handtuch schlagen, damit kein Dampf aus dem Topf entweichen kann. So für ca. 30 min dämpfen.
- Safran in etwas warmem Wasser anrühren, bis sich das Wasser rot färbt. Danach eine Schüssel vom fertigen Reis nehmen und das Safran-Wasser darüber geben, damit sich der Reis satt gelb färbt. Am Ende den gelben und den weißen Reis miteinander vermischen.

How to prepare the Gorme Badenjan:

- Peel the aubergines and cut into 5 mm thick slices. Heat plenty of oil and fry the aubergines until they are golden brown; then set aside.
- Grate the onions and the garlic and process to viscous mass; add the sieved tomatoes and season with salt, pepper, and curry.
- Peel the potatoes and cut into 5 mm thick slices. Put oil in a large cooking pot and cover the bottom of the cooking pot with potato slices. Then, layer the aubergines and the tomato sauce by turns over the potatoes.
  Simmer for approximately 20 min on low.

How to prepare the rice:

- Soak the rice for 3 h in cold water. Pour out the water and put the rice with 6 cups of fresh water on the stove.
- Cook the rice for approximately 15 min, until it still has some bite. Pour out the water. Put some oil in a Teflon pan, add the rice and cook on low. Wrap the lid into a towel so that no steam can escape. Steam the rice for approximately 30 min.
- Mix the saffron with some warm water until the water turns red. Extract one bowl of the finished rice and douse with the saffron water so that it turns yellow. Before serving, mix the white and the yellow rice.

45

HAVIJ

AFGHANISTAN

1 Bund Karotten
1 bunch of carrots

1 Bund Petersilie
1 bunch of parsley

1 Bund Koriander
1 bunch of coriander

1 Bund Minze
1 bunch of mint

2 Zwiebeln
2 onions

4 Knoblauchzehen
4 cloves of garlic

250 g rote Linsen
250 g red lentils

1 Dose Tomaten
1 can of tomatoes

Salz, Pfeffer, Currypulver
salt, pepper, curry powder

dieses Gericht ist vegan
this dish is vegan

CREMIG-LEICHTE GEMÜSESUPPE

LIGHT AND CREAMY VEGETABLE SOUP

- Karotten schälen und in kleine Würfel schneiden. Die Blätter von den Kräutern zupfen und fein hacken.
- Die Zwiebeln und den Knoblauch sehr fein hacken.
- Die Linsen waschen und mit den Karotten in einen Topf mit etwa 2 l Wasser geben.
- Sobald das Wasser kocht, die Tomaten, den Knoblauch und die Zwiebeln in den Topf geben.
- Mit Salz, Pfeffer und Currypulver abschmecken.
- Etwa 20 min kochen lassen, dann vom Herd nehmen und die gehackten Kräuter dazugeben.
- Zum Schluss die Suppe pürieren und servieren.

- Peel the carrots and chop into small pieces; finely chop the herbs.
- Chop onions and garlic into small pieces.
- Wash the lentils and put them together with the carrots in a cooking pot with 2 l water.
- Once the water is boiling, add tomatoes, onions, and garlic.
- Season with salt, pepper, and curry powder.
- Cook for approximately 20 min, set the cooking pot aside and add the herbs.
- Puree the soup and serve.

REZA

Rezas Familie kommt ursprünglich aus Afghanistan, doch er selbst wurde im Iran geboren und verbrachte dort seine Kindheit. In seiner Heimat absolvierte Reza eine Ausbildung zum Schuhmacher. Mit 21 Jahren musste er sein Land verlassen und schlug sich zunächst über die Türkei bis nach Griechenland durch. Dort arbeitete er, um genug Geld für ein Flugticket in die Niederlande zu sparen. In den Niederlanden wurde Reza für ein Jahr und zwei Monate ins Gefängnis eingewiesen. Dieses durfte er nur unter der Auflage verlassen, dass er auch das Land verlässt. Nach einem kurzen Aufenthalt in Norwegen musste er zurück nach Holland und wurde von dort nach Afghanistan abgeschoben. Von Afghanistan aus lief er zu Fuß in den Iran und dann weiter über seine alte Route in die Türkei und nach Griechenland. Seit etwas mehr als einem Jahr versucht er nun sein Glück in Deutschland. Inzwischen ist er 28 und seit mehr als sieben Jahren auf der Flucht. Hier versucht er Normalität in sein Leben zu bringen. Er geht täglich zum Deutschunterricht und spricht die Sprache bereits fließend. Zweimal pro Woche geht er in einen Schachboxverein, in dem er sich bereits ein großes Netzwerk an Freunden aufbauen konnte. Sein Traum ist es eine Ausbildung zum Altenpfleger zu machen, um hier eine Arbeit und ein neues Zuhause zu finden.

Jenny, Rezas Kochpartnerin

Reza's family is originally from Afghanistan but he was born and grew up in Iran. In his home country, Reza did an apprenticeship as a shoemaker. At the age of 21 he had to leave Iran and made his way to Greece, via Turkey. It was in Greece that he worked so he could raise money for a plane ticket to the Netherlands. There he was sent to prison for 14 months. He was only allowed to leave the prison under the condition that he also leaves the country. After a short stay in Norway he had to return to Holland and was deported back to Afghanistan. From Afghanistan he walked to Iran and from there, his journey took him via Turkey and Greece to Germany.
At the age of 28, after seven years of restless travelling, he finally arrived in a country where he can stay. Every day Reza attends German classes and is already fluent. He goes to a chess-boxing club twice a week and has already built up a large network of friends. His dream is to start an apprenticeship as a carer for the elderly, to find a job and a new home.

Jenny, Reza's cooking partner

CHICKEN CURRY

ANEES

40

CHICKEN CURRY

PAKISTAN

1 kg Hähnchenschenkel
1 kg chicken drumsticks

3 Zwiebeln
3 onions

3 Tomaten
3 tomatoes

50 g Ingwer
50 g ginger

30 g Knoblauch
30 g garlic

1 Bund Koriander
1 bunch of coriander

3 TL Curry (gemahlen)
3 tsp curry powder

3 Kardamomsamen
3 cardamom seeds

204

204

½ TL Garam Masala
½ tsp garam masala

6 Nelken
6 cloves

Salz, Pfeffer,
200 ml Pflanzenöl
salt, pepper,
200 ml vegetable oil

Naan oder arabisches Brot
Naan or Arabic bread

KNUSPRIGE HÄHNCHENSCHENKEL
CRISPY CHICKEN DRUMSTICKS

- Ingwer und Knoblauch zu einer Paste pürieren, Hähnchen waschen, Tomaten und Zwiebeln zerkleinern.
- Öl in einer Pfanne erhitzen. Zwiebeln bei mittlerer Hitze anbraten, bis sie goldbraun sind.
- Tomaten, Ingwer-Knoblauch-Paste, Hähnchen und die Gewürze (außer Garam Masala) hinzufügen.
- Alles für 10 min braten. Anschließend 400 ml Wasser hinzufügen und auf mittlerer Hitze köcheln lassen, bis das Hähnchen gar ist.
- Nun etwas Garam Masala und frischen Koriander auf das Hähnchen streuen und weitere 5 min köcheln lassen.
- Das Hähnchencurry mit etwas Brot servieren (Naan oder arabisches Brot).

- Grind ginger and garlic to a thick paste, wash the chicken, chop tomatoes and onions.
- Heat oil in a pan. Add the onions and fry until golden.
- Add tomatoes, ginger and garlic paste, chicken and spices – except garam masala.
- Leave the mixture to fry for 10 min. Then add 400 ml of water and cook on medium heat until chicken is tender.
- Now, sprinkle some garam masala and fresh coriander leaves on the chicken curry and let it simmer for 5 min.
- Serve the chicken curry with some bread (Naan or Arabic bread).

HIER IN DEUTSCHLAND FÜHLE ICH MICH SICHER.

Anees

HERE IN GERMANY I FEEL SAFE.

Anees

ANEES

Anees ist bereits viel herumgekommen. Nachdem er seine Heimatstadt Lahore in Pakistan verließ, lebte er fünf Jahre in Spanien und lernte dort neben Land und Leuten auch die spanische Sprache kennen. In Spanien jobbte Anees in Restaurants und schaute sich von den Köchen viel ab. „In Pakistan habe ich nie gekocht – ich wusste gar nicht, wie das geht", verrät er mir. In den letzten Jahren ist er zu einem richtigen Kochprofi geworden. Sein „Chicken Curry" ist das beste, das ich je gegessen habe. Um bessere Arbeitsverhältnisse zu finden, beschloss Anees weiterzuziehen. Vor drei Jahren kam er nach Berlin und lebte zunächst für zwei Jahre in einem Asylheim. Deutschland gefällt Anees gut. „Hier in Deutschland fühle ich mich sicher und vielleicht finde ich ja auch noch eine Frau." Auf die Frage, wie er die Menschen in Deutschland findet, sagt er: „In jedem Land gibt es nette und unfreundliche Menschen, das ist doch überall gleich. Mensch ist Mensch."
Ich finde, damit hat Anees recht!

Lisa, Anees' Kochpartnerin

Anees has lived in many different places since leaving his hometown of Lahore in Pakistan. He lived in Spain for five years where he came to know the people, the culture, and also the Spanish language. Anees used to work in different restaurants and learned many things from the Spanish chefs just by watching. "In Pakistan, I never cooked – I did not know how to", he explained. However, during the last years he has become a real professional chef. His "Chicken Curry" was the best curry I have ever tried.
In order to find better working conditions, Anees decided to move on. Three years ago he came to Berlin and first lived in an asylum home for two years. Anees really likes Germany. "Here in Germany I feel safe and maybe I will even find a wife." When asked how he likes the Germans he says: "In every country there are nice and rude people and that's the same everywhere. People are people."
I can totally agree with that.

Lisa, Anees' cooking partner

ULA

TABOULEH

10

TABOULEH

SYRIEN · SYRIA

203

1 Tasse Bulgur
1 cup of bulgur

2 gr. Tomaten
2 large tomatoes

2 Bund glatte Petersilie
2 bunches of flat leaf parsley

½ Kopfsalat oder Romanasalat
½ head lettuce or romaine lettuce

getrocknete Minze
dried mint

Kreuzkümmel
cumin

Olivenöl
olive oil

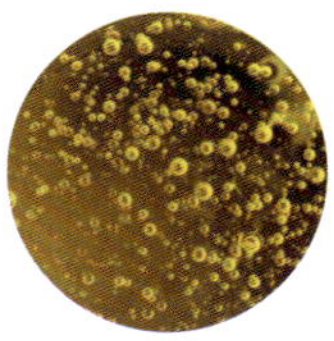

Saft von 2 Zitronen
juice of 2 lemons

Salz, Pfeffer
salt, pepper

dieses Gericht ist vegan
this dish is vegan

FRISCHER BULGURSALAT MIT MINZE
FRESH BULGUR SALAD WITH MINT

- Den Bulgur in 1½ Tassen kochendem Wasser und dem Zitronensaft quellen lassen. Anschließend reichlich Olivenöl hinzufügen.
- Die Tomaten fein würfeln. Minze, Petersilie und Kopfsalat fein schneiden und alles vermengen.
- Mit Salz, Pfeffer und Kreuzkümmel würzen und beiseitestellen.
- Erst kurz vor dem Essen den Bulgur und die Tomaten-Petersilie-Mischung miteinander vermengen.

- Soak the bulgur in 1½ cups of hot water and lemon juice. Then add plenty of olive oil.
- Chop the tomatoes and the lettuce into small pieces, hash parsley and mint, and mix everything.
- Season with salt, pepper, and cumin, then set aside.
- Mix the bulgur and tomato-parsley mixture just before eating.

ULA

Ula stammt aus Damaskus in Syrien. Dort lebte sie, bis sie im Oktober 2013 mit ihren drei Kindern nach Deutschland kam. Seit ein paar Monaten lebt nun auch ihr Mann mit ihnen hier. Ihre Eltern und ihre Geschwister halten sich allerdings immer noch in Syrien auf. Ula vermisst sie daher sehr.
In Deutschland gefällt es ihr trotzdem bisher sehr gut. Es gibt vieles, das neu für sie ist, zum Beispiel, dass es sehr viele Papiere für Anträge und Ähnliches gibt und dass man für alles einen Termin vereinbaren muss. Das war in Syrien anders. Auch Pünktlichkeit spielte dort nicht so eine große Rolle wie hier. „Aber das hat auch seine guten Seiten", findet sie. Dadurch ist vieles besser organisiert.
Was sie sowohl in Deutschland als auch in Syrien gerne macht ist Kochen. Vor allem liebt sie die palästinensische Küche. Ihr Lieblingsgericht sind kleine, mit Nüssen und Datteln gefüllte Gebäckstücke mit Zimt und Ingwer. Sie hat aber auch noch viele andere Köstlichkeiten in ihrem Repertoire, wie zum Beispiel das leckere „Tabouleh".

Conny, Ulas Kochpartnerin

Ula comes from Damascus, Syria, where she lived until October 2013 before coming to Germany with her three children. Ula's husband has also been living with the family in Germany for the last few months. Ula's parents and her siblings are still living in Syria and she misses them a lot.
However, she really likes Germany so far. She is learning to deal with many new things as she transitions from living in Syria to living in Germany, such as the many forms she must fill out and the various appointments she must attend. This is a complete contrast to life in Syria where punctuality does not play such an important role. While this adjustment has been challenging, it has good sides, too, she thinks. Everything in Germany is better organised. One thing she likes to do both in Germany and Syria is to cook. She especially likes Palestinian cuisine. Her favourite dish is small pastries filled with nuts and dates and seasoned with cinnamon and ginger. She has also many other delicacies in her repertoire, such as her delicious "Tabouleh".

Conny, Ula's cooking partner

BIHARI KABAB
BLACK DHAL
PAKORAS

SHAIKH

50 + 12 H

CHICKEN BIHARI KABAB

PAKISTAN

800 g Hähnchenbrust
800 g chicken breast

1 Bund frischer Koriander
1 bunch of fresh coriander

2 Zitronen (unbehandelt)
2 lemons (untreated)

1 Zwiebel
1 onion

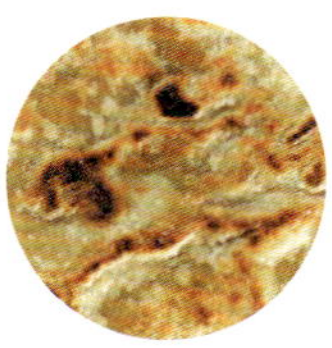
pakistanisches Brot oder Paratha
Pakistani bread or paratha 206

für die Marinade · for the marinade

60 g Joghurt
60 g yoghurt

50 g Knoblauch
50 g garlic

30 g Ingwer
30 g ginger

2 TL Chili (gemahlen)
2 tsp chili powder

1 TL Koriander (gemahlen)
1 tsp coriander powder

½ EL Garam masala
½ tbsp garam masala 204

1 Messerspitze grüner Kardamom (gemahlen)
1 pinch of green cardamom powder 204

1 EL Melonenkerne
1 tbsp melon seeds 205

1 TL Kreuzkümmel (gemahlen)
1 tsp cumin powder

1 Prise Salz, 1 Prise schwarzer Pfeffer
1 pinch of salt, 1 pinch of black pepper

SCHARFES PAKISTANISCHES HÄHNCHEN

SPICY PAKISTANI CHICKEN

Marinieren:

- Ingwer und Knoblauch schälen und mit etwas Wasser in einem Gefäß pürieren.
- Alle Gewürze und den Joghurt hinzufügen, gut vermengen.
- Das Hähnchen waschen und in grobe Stücke schneiden. Die Hähnchenstücke in eine große Schüssel geben und die Gewürz-Joghurt-Paste dazugeben. Gut vermengen und über Nacht im Kühlschrank ruhen lassen.

Backen:

- Den Ofen auf 250° (Umluft) vorheizen.
- Das marinierte Hähnchen auf einem Backblech verteilen und 30 min backen. Anschließend die Hähnchenstücke einmal wenden und weitere 20 min backen. Falls das Hähnchen zu dunkel wird, mit Alufolie abdecken.
- Die Zwiebel und die Zitronen in dünne Scheiben schneiden.
- Hähnchen aus dem Ofen nehmen und mit Zwiebelstreifen, Zitronenscheiben und frischem Koriander garnieren.
- Mit Brot servieren.

Marinate:

- Peel ginger and garlic and grind with a little bit of water.
- Add all spices and yoghurt, mix well.
- Wash the chicken and cut into roughly chopped pieces. Add chicken into a big bowl and mix with the spice-yoghurt-paste. Mix well and leave overnight in the fridge.

Bake:

- Preheat the oven at 250° (convection oven).
- Spread the marinated chicken on a baking tray. Bake for 30 min then turn the chicken and bake again in the oven for 20 min. If the chicken turns dark, cover with aluminium foil.
- Take chicken out of the oven and garnish with onion slices, pieces of lemon and fresh coriander.
- Serve with bread.

90

BLACK DHAL

PAKISTAN

400 g schwarze Linsen
400 g black lentils

1 Tasse Reis
1 cup of rice

1½ frische grüne Chilischoten
1½ fresh green chilis

1 kl. Zwiebel
1 small onion

204

125 g Butter oder Ghee
125 g butter or ghee

2 Knoblauchzehen
2 cloves of garlic

1 TL Kurkuma
1 tsp curcuma

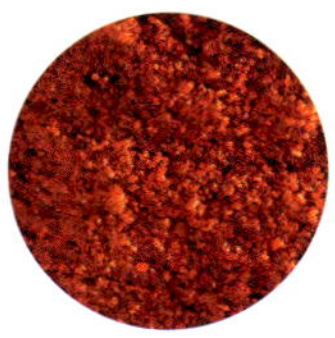

1 TL Chilipulver
1 tsp chili powder

½ Bund frischer Koriander
½ bunch of fresh coriander

statt Ghee Pflanzenmargarine verwenden
use vegetable margarine instead of ghee

SCHWARZER LINSENEINTOPF
BLACK LENTIL STEW

- Die Linsen zwei- bis dreimal gründlich waschen. Anschließend in einen Topf mit ¾ l gesalzenem Wasser geben. Die Linsen zum Kochen bringen.
- Chilischoten in feine Ringe schneiden und nach 15 min zusammen mit dem Chili- und Kurkumapulver zu den kochenden Linsen geben.
- In einer Pfanne Butter oder Ghee erhitzen. Zwiebeln und Knoblauch klein schneiden und in der Pfanne goldbraun braten.
- 1 Tasse Reis mit der doppelten Menge gesalzenem Wasser zum Kochen bringen und gar kochen lassen (ca. 20 min). Wenn der Reis noch nicht gar, das ganze Wasser aber bereits verkocht ist, ein wenig Wasser hinzugeben.
- Nach 40 min die Linsen vom Herd nehmen und den gebratenen Knoblauch-Zwiebel-Mix untermengen.
- Die Linsen zusammen mit Reis und frischem Koriander servieren.

- Wash lentils two to three times and pour into a large pot. Add ¾ l salted water and bring everything to boil.
- Cut chilis and add to the cooking dhal after 15 min. Also add curcuma and chili powder.
- Heat ghee or butter in a pan. Cut onion and garlic into small pieces. Fry in the pan until golden.
- Bring 1 cup of rice and 2 cups of salted water to boil in a big pot. Boil for 20 min until soft. If needed, add a little bit of water.
- After 40 min, add fried garlic and onion to the lentils and stir well.
- Serve lentils with rice and fresh coriander.

90 + 3 H

PAKORAS

PAKISTAN

205

250 g Kichererbsenmehl
250 g chickpea flour

1½ TL Koriandersamen
1½ tsp coriander seeds

1½ TL ganzer Kümmel
1½ tsp whole cumin

1 TL Chilipulver
1 tsp chili powder

2 gr. Kartoffeln
2 big potatoes

½ Bund frischer Spinat mit großen Blättern
½ bunch of fresh spinach with big leaves

1 Zwiebel
1 onion

100 ml Sonnenblumenöl
100 ml sunflower oil

dieses Gericht ist vegan
this dish is vegan

- Die Gewürze zusammen mit dem Kichererbsenmehl in einer großen Schüssel gut vermengen. Anschließend Wasser hinzugeben, bis ein dicker, glatter Teig entsteht. Wichtig ist, dass dieser nicht zu flüssig ist.
- Den Teig für 2 – 3 h bei Raumtemperatur abgedeckt ruhen lassen.
- Die Kartoffeln und die Zwiebeln in sehr dünne Scheiben schneiden. Die Spinatblätter abzupfen und waschen.
- Öl in einer Pfanne erhitzen. Nacheinander Kartoffel-, Zwiebelscheiben oder Spinatblätter in den Pakorateig tauchen und anschließend in das heiße Öl geben. Die Pakoras sollten im Öl schwimmen, ggf. also mehr Öl dazugeben.
- Die Pakoras auf einer Seite braten, bis sie eine leicht bräunliche Farbe bekommen. Anschließend umdrehen und schließlich auf einem Teller mit Küchenpapier abtropfen und etwas abkühlen lassen.
- Warm servieren.

GEFÜLLTE TEIGTASCHEN AUS KICHERERBSENMEHL
FRITTERS MADE FROM CHICKPEA FLOUR

- Mix the spices and the chickpea flour together in a big bowl. Afterwards, add water and stir until a medium thick batter is formed. Take care that the batter does not become too runny.
- Leave the batter covered for approximately 2 – 3 h at room temperature.
- Cut onions and potatoes into very thin slices. Wash the spinach and take off a handful of big leaves.
- Heat oil in a pan. One after another, dip the potato, onion, and spinach pieces into the batter and subsequently fry them in the hot oil.
- Fry pakoras on each side until golden. Leave pakoras to dry and cool on a plate covered with paper towels.
- Serve warm.

SHAIKH

Shaikh – manch einem mag er vielleicht bekannt vorkommen – ist 44 Jahre alt und lebt seit Juni 2013 in Berlin. Bereits letztes Jahr verriet er uns ein Rezept für unser erstes Kochbuch. Seither ist er fester Bestandteil des Über den Tellerrand kochen-Teams und stellt in den von ihm geleiteten Kochkursen die pakistanische Küche vor. Er kennt neben den außergewöhnlichen Geschmackskombinationen auch die heilenden und wohltuenden Wirkungen vieler Zutaten. Diese präsentiert er in den Kursen immer auf eine interessante, aber auch unterhaltsame Weise. „Ich möchte meine Leidenschaft für's Kochen teilen", sagt er.
Durch die Kochkurse hat Shaikh schon viele Kontakte geknüpft und Freunde gefunden. Trotzdem vermisst er oft seine Familie. „Niemand verlässt freiwillig seine Heimat. Es sind schwerwiegende Gründe, die dich dazu zwingen", sagt Shaikh. Zu seiner Familie in Karatschi hat er nach wie vor nur wenig Kontakt. Bei der Frage, was er brauche, muss er daher lachen: Seine Frau und seine Kinder könne ihm keiner ersetzen. „Was mir Angst macht, ist, dass man als Flüchtling nie weiß, was einen als nächstes erwartet", erzählt Shaikh. Aber er tut alles, um sich in Berlin weiterhin eine Zukunft aufzubauen.

Caro, Shaikhs Kochpartnerin

Shaikh – some of you might remember him– is 44 years old and has been living in Berlin since June 2013. Last year he already shared one of his recipes with us in our first cookbook. Since then he is part of the Über den Tellerrand kochen team. Regularly, he presents the Pakistani cuisine in our cooking classes. He not only knows about extraordinary combinations of different tastes but also about the health benefits of many ingredients. In his cooking classes he always shares his knowledge in an interesting but also entertaining way. "I would like to share my passion for cooking", he says.
Through the cooking classes he already managed to socialise quite a bit and found new friends. Nevertheless he often misses his family. "Nobody wants to leave his home country, so there must be serious reasons, that make you go away", says Shaikh. He does not have much contact to his family in Karachi. That is why he has to laugh when he is being asked what he needs: nobody can replace his family. Shaikh says that sometimes he is afraid because as a refugee one never knows what to expect next. However, he keeps on trying his best to create a positive future for himself in Berlin.

Caro, Shaikh's cooking partner

MUHI & HOSAMA

MOJEDERA

20

MOJEDERA

SYRIEN · SYRIA

203

1 Tasse Bulgur
1 cup of bulgur

100 g grüne Linsen (eingeweicht)
100 g green lentils (pre-soaked)

1 Zwiebel
1 onion

3 Tomaten
3 tomatoes

Olivenöl
olive oil

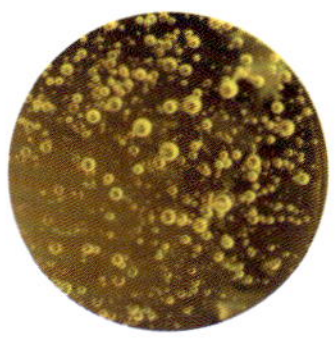

Salz, Pfeffer
salt, pepper

dieses Gericht ist vegan
this dish is vegan

LINSEN-BULGUR-MIX
LENTILS AND BULGUR

- Bulgur in 2 – 3 Tassen Wasser auf höchster Stufe zum Kochen bringen und dann auf die kleinste Stufe stellen.
- Die Linsen abtropfen lassen, in einen Topf geben, mit Wasser bedecken und 5 – 10 min kochen.
- Die Linsen abschütten und mit dem Bulgur mischen. Mit Salz, Pfeffer und 2 EL Olivenöl abschmecken.
- Klein geschnittene Zwiebeln in Olivenöl glasig anbraten. Das Bulgur-Linsen-Gemisch auf einem Teller anrichten und die Zwiebeln darauf verteilen. Dazu frische Tomaten servieren.

- Add 2 – 3 cups of water to the bulgur and bring to boil, then reduce the heat to the lowest possible level.
- Discard the soaking water from the lentils, cover with the water in a pot and cook for 5 – 10 min.
- Mix the lentils with the bulgur. Season with salt, pepper, and 2 tbsp olive oil.
- Finely chop the onion and fry in olive oil in a separate pan. Pour the bulgur-lentil mixture onto a plate, ladle the fried onions on top and garnish with freshly chopped tomato.

SN
OW

Ich habe mit einer Familie aus Syrien gekocht. Der Vater heißt Muhi und ist 39 Jahre alt, er hat in Syrien in der Pharmaindustrie gearbeitet. Die Mutter heißt Hosama, sie ist 38 Jahre alt und war Journalistin. Sie leben seit Juni 2014 in Deutschland.
Über ihr Leben in Syrien reden sie kaum.
Die drei Söhne sind sieben, neun und elf Jahre alt und gehen mittlerweile hier zur Schule. Die Familie wird von der *Caritas* betreut und hat zwei Helfer von der Organisation *Sprache verbindet*. Außerdem beginnt bald ein Deutschkurs für die Eltern.

Lena, Muhis und Hosamas Kochpartnerin

I cooked with a Syrian family. The father is called Muhi and is 39 years old and comes from Syria. He and his family have been living in Germany since June 2014. In Syria, Muhi used to work in the pharmaceutical industry. His wife Hosama, who is 38 years old, used to be a journalist. They rarely talk about their life in Syria. Muhi and Hosama have three sons who are aged seven, nine and eleven; the children all attend school. The family is supported by the charity *Caritas* and are connected with two helpers from the organisation *Sprache verbindet*. Muhi and Hosama will soon be participating in German classes.

Lena, Muhi's and Hosama's cooking partner

CHASHUSHULI

EKA

CHASHUSHULI

GEORGIEN · GEORGIA

60

500 g Rindergulasch
500 g stewing beef

400 g frische Champignons
400 g fresh mushrooms

3 Zwiebeln
3 onions

2 Knoblauchzehen
2 cloves of garlic

½ Bund frischer Dill
½ bunch of fresh dill

200 g türkischer Hartkäse (45%)
200 g Turkish hard cheese (45%)

1 kl. Glas Mayonnaise
1 small jar of mayonnaise

Sonnenblumenöl
sunflower oil

Salz, Pfeffer, Paprikapulver
salt, pepper, paprika powder

einige Blätter frische Minze
a few leaves of fresh mint

TRADITIONELLER AUFLAUF
TRADITIONAL CASSEROLE

- Zwiebeln fein würfeln, Knoblauch und Dill fein hacken. Dann alles beiseitestellen.
- In einer Pfanne etwas Öl erhitzen, das Gulasch hinzufügen und auf kleiner Flamme unter ständigem Wenden garen. Wenn das Fleisch gar ist, die Zwiebeln und (etwas später) den Knoblauch zufügen und glasig dünsten.
- Das Fleisch aus der Pfanne nehmen und in eine Auflaufform füllen. Mit Pfeffer abschmecken.
- In einer anderen Pfanne etwas Öl erhitzen und bei hoher Temperatur die Champignons garen, bis sie weich und braun sind.
- Die Champignons und den Dill zu dem Fleisch geben und alles gut vermengen. Gut mit Salz, Pfeffer und Paprikapulver würzen.
- Die Masse glattstreichen. Den Käse mit einer groben Reibe reiben und auf dem Fleisch verteilen. Anschließend die Mayonnaise über den Auflauf streichen und mit einigen Blättern Minze verzieren.
- Den Auflauf bei 200° im Backofen (Ober-/Unterhitze) auf der mittleren Schiene für 20 min garen.

- Finely chop the onions, the dill, and the garlic into small pieces. Chop the dill and put to one side.
- Heat some oil in a pan, add the beef and cook on low while stirring constantly. When the meat is cooked, add the onions and fry briefly before adding the garlic.
- Place the meat mixture into a casserole dish and season with pepper.
- Heat some oil in a pan and fry the mushrooms on high until they are brown and softened.
- Combine the mushrooms with the meat and the dill, season everything with salt, pepper, and paprika powder.
- Grate the cheese and sprinkle over the meat. Spread the mayonnaise on top and decorate with some mint leaves.
- Bake the casserole for 20 min at 200° (top and bottom heating).

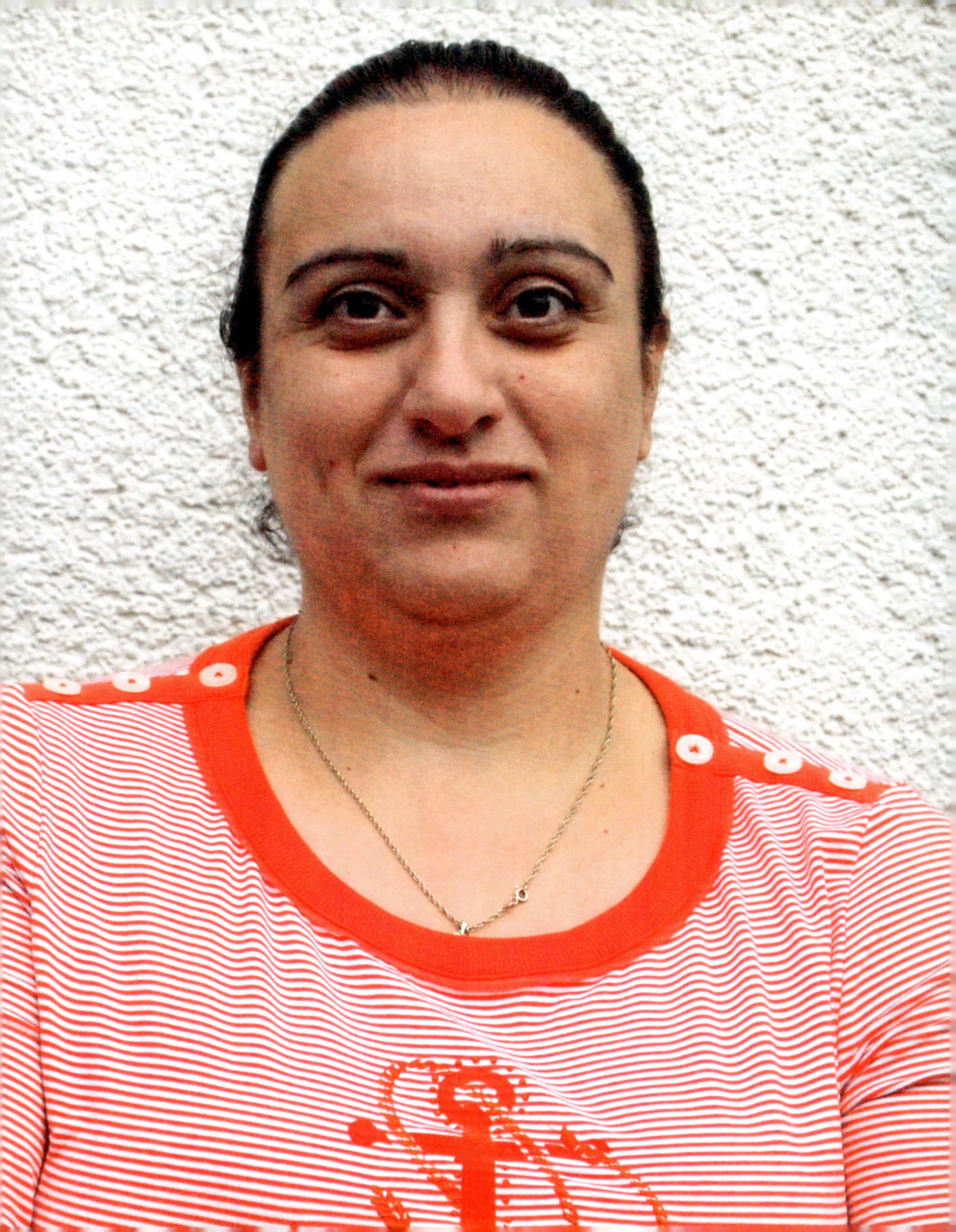

Ein Jahr und neun Monate ist es her, dass die 28-jährige Eka mit ihrem Mann und ihrem 8-jährigen Sohn aus politischen Gründen von Tiflis, Georgien, nach Deutschland kam. Nach einem kurzen Aufenthalt in Schöppingen landeten sie in Bochum.
Obwohl sie bisher noch nicht sehr viele Kontakte geknüpft haben, fühlen sie sich in der neuen Heimat schon sehr wohl, vor allem sehr sicher.
Ihr Wunsch ist, über Kontakte zu Deutschen und mit privaten Deutschkursen schnell ihre Sprachkenntnisse zu verbessern, um sich so eine Grundlage für eine Zukunft in Deutschland zu schaffen.
Das von Eka gekochte Chashushuli gehört zu den typisch georgischen Gerichten und existiert in vielen Varianten. Es ist ein Gericht, das man gerne bestellt, wenn man in ein Restaurant geht oder etwas für Familienfeiern zubereitet. Es wird in Georgien meistens in vielen kleinen Auflaufformen serviert und nicht in einer großen.

Claudia, Ekas Kochpartnerin

It has been a year and nine months since 28 year old Eka, her husband and their 8 year old son left Tiflis, Georgia, due to political reasons and fled to Germany. After a short stay in Schöppingen, the three of them moved to Bochum.
Although they have not yet made many friends in their new home, the small family feels comfortable and, most importantly, safe. One of their biggest dreams is to improve their language skills through socialising with Germans and by attending private German lessons. In this way they hope to form a solid base in order to ensure a happy future in Germany.
The Chashushuli that Eka cooked is a typical Georgian dish that exists in various forms. It is a dish that can be ordered in a restaurant or prepared for family celebrations. In Georgia, Chashushuli is served in small casserole dishes rather than just one large one.

Claudia, Eka's cooking partner

LUIZA

CHINGALSCH

40

CHINGALSCH

TSCHETSCHENIEN · CHECHNYA

1 Hokkaidokürbis
1 Hokkaido pumpkin

1 kg Mehl
1 kg flour

500 ml Milch
500 ml milk

½ EL Backsoda
½ tbsp baking soda

½ EL Zucker
½ tbsp sugar

Butter
butter

1 Prise Salz, ½ EL Pfeffer, Pflanzenöl
1 pinch of salt, ½ tbsp pepper, vegetable oil

statt Milch Sojamilch, statt Butter Pflanzenmargarine verwenden
use soya milk instead of milk; vegetable margarine instead of butter

DÜNNE KÜRBISTEIGTASCHEN
DELICATE PUMPKIN PARCELS

- Mehl, Milch, Backsoda und Salz zu einem Teig verarbeiten. Kleine Kugeln formen und zu einem dünnen Fladen ausrollen.
- Den Kürbis in Stücke schneiden, 15 – 20 min kochen, zerdrücken und mit Zucker und Pfeffer abschmecken.
- Die Kürbismasse jeweils auf die Hälfte eines Fladens streichen, die andere Hälfte darüber klappen. Dann erneut vorsichtig ausrollen.
- Im Backofen oder in einer heißen, mit Pflanzenöl eingefetteten Pfanne ca. 20 min ausbacken. Zum Schluss mit Butter bestreichen.

- Combine flour, milk, baking soda, and salt to a dough. Form small balls and roll out into thin pancakes.
- Cut the pumpkin into small pieces, boil for 15 – 20 min, mash and season with sugar and pepper.
- Place the mashed pumpkin onto half of a pancake and fold the other half over it, roll out again.
- Bake for 20 min in the oven or in a pan with oil, then brush with butter.

ESSEN VERBINDET UND BRINGT VERSCHIEDENE KULTUREN AN EINEN TISCH.

Luiza

EATING CONNECTS AND BRINGS TOGETHER MANY CULTURES TO ONE TABLE.

Luiza

Luiza kommt aus Tschetschenien, jetzt lebt sie in Luckenwalde. Kochen hat sie von ihrer Mutter gelernt. Als sie mit 15 heiratete, musste sie sich aber alles Weitere selbst beibringen. Meistens kocht sie typische Gerichte aus ihrer Heimat. Sie hat aber auch schon ein paar neue Dinge probiert. „Es war sehr lustig, als ich Ketchup das erste Mal probiert habe – er war süß! Bei uns ist er immer salzig. Ich war sehr überrascht", erzählt sie.
Einige Kontakte in Deutschland konnte Luiza schon schließen, zum Beispiel während der Gruppentreffen des Vereins *KommMit – für Migranten und Flüchtlinge e.V.*, der sich insbesondere für die Flüchtlingsfrauen in Luckenwalde einsetzt und sie unterstützt. Dort lernte sie auch viele Speisen aus unterschiedlichen Ländern kennen, denn unter der Trägerschaft des Vereins initiierten Studentinnen der Humboldt-Universität zu Berlin das Projekt *Nordkaukasische Köstlichkeiten.* Zusammen mit einigen der Flüchtlingsfrauen in Luckenwalde entstand ein kleines Rezeptbuch. Das Projekt hat sowohl Luiza als auch den Studentinnen gut gefallen, denn „Essen verbindet und bringt verschiedene Kulturen an einen Tisch" – da sind sie sich einig!

Annika und Tina, Luizas Kochpartnerinnen

Luiza comes from Chechnya but now lives in Luckenwalde. Her mother taught her how to cook. When she got married at the age of 15, Luiza had to learn everything else on her own. She usually cooks regional dishes from her home country. However, she has begun to try a few new things. "It was really funny, the first time I've tried ketchup here it tasted sweet but back home the taste of ketchup is always salty! I was very surprised", she tells.
Luiza has already been able to make some contacts through the group meetings of a club called *KommMit – für Migranten und Flüchtlinge e.V.*. This organisation focuses on supporting and working with refugees.
It was at these meetings that she became acquainted with diverse dishes from different countries. With the sponsorship of the club and in cooperation with students of the Humboldt University Berlin, a small recipe book has already been created.
Luiza and the students really liked the project because "eating connects and brings together many cultures to one table".

Annika und Tina, Luiza's cooking partners

KEEMA MATAR

SULEMAN

40

KEEMA MATAR

PAKISTAN

Arabisches Brot
Arabic bread

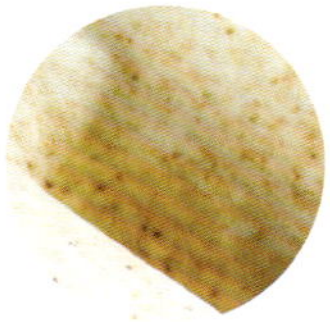

500 g Lammhackfleisch (Keema)
500 g minced lamb meat (keema)

250 g Erbsen, 2 Tomaten
250 g shelled peas, 2 tomatoes

1 Zwiebel, 2 TL pürierter Knoblauch
1 onion, 2 tsp garlic paste

1½ TL pürierter Ingwer
1½ tsp ginger paste

1 TL gemahlener Kreuzkümmel
1 tsp cumin powder

½ TL gemahlene Kurkuma
½ tsp curcuma powder

6 Nelken
6 cloves

1 TL gemahlener Koriander
1 tsp coriander powder

1 TL Garam Masala
1 tsp garam masala

204

½ Bund frischer Koriander
½ bunch of fresh coriander

2 TL Pflanzenöl, ½ TL Chilipulver, 6 TL Salz
2 tsp vegetable oil, ½ tsp chili powder, 6 tsp salt

statt Lammfleisch Sojafleisch verwenden
use soya meat instead of lamb

KRÄFTIGER LAMM-ERBSEN-EINTOPF
AROMATIC LAMB AND PEA STEW

- Die Zwiebel in schmale Streifen schneiden, Tomaten in Stückchen hacken und aus Knoblauch und Ingwer eine Paste mischen.
- Das Öl in einer Pfanne erhitzen und anschließend die Zwiebeln darin anschwitzen, bis sie eine bräunliche Farbe haben.
- Die Ingwer-Knoblauch-Paste, den Kreuzkümmel, das Kurkuma- und das Chilipulver sowie die Nelken in die Pfanne geben und gut in das Öl einrühren. Danach das Garam Masala dazugeben und warten, bis das Öl an die Oberfläche steigt.
- Nun das Hackfleisch, die Tomaten und das Salz dazugeben und für 10 min braten. Danach mit etwas Wasser ablöschen.
- Die Erbsen hinzufügen und das Ganze mit geschlossenem Deckel bei geringer Hitze köcheln lassen, bis das Hackfleisch und die Erbsen gar sind. Gegebenenfalls zwischendurch etwas Wasser hinzugeben.
- Nun die Hackfleischsoße mit dem Korianderpulver bestreuen und zuletzt mit etwas frischem Koriander garnieren.
- Das arabische Brot erwärmen und mit Keema Matar servieren.

- Chop the onions into small strips and the tomatoes into small pieces; mix the garlic and ginger together to make a paste.
- Heat oil in a pan and sauté the onions until they turn brown.
- Add the ginger-garlic paste, cumin, curcuma, chili, and cloves and stir well; afterwards add the garam masala and wait until the oil has raised to the surface.
- Add the minced meat, tomatoes and salt; fry for 10 min then deglaze with some water.
- Add the peas and let everything simmer with a closed lid until the meat and the peas are cooked; add water in between if necessary.
- Sprinkle with coriander powder and garnish with fresh coriander.
- Heat the Arabic bread and serve together with Keema Matar.

SULEMAN

Vor etwas mehr als einem Jahr kam Suleman aus Pakistan (Islamabad) nach Deutschland. Seitdem lebt er in einem Asylheim in Marienfelde – am Stadtrand von Berlin. Suleman liebt die deutsche Hauptstadt. „Berlin ist so bunt und noch dazu total günstig. Hier möchte ich bleiben“, erzählt er lächelnd. Zuvor hatte er bereits zwei Jahre in London bei seiner älteren Schwester gelebt – aber gefallen hatte es ihm dort nicht so richtig. „Es ist teuer, voll und es gibt wenige Möglichkeiten ein gutes Leben zu führen.“

Hier in Deutschland teilt sich der 29-jährige Suleman ein Zimmer mit einem netten Pakistaner. Außerdem hat er bereits viele Freunde gewonnen, die mit ihm ein ähnliches Schicksal teilen. Als wir uns zum Kochen trafen, brachte er seinen Freund Mohammed mit, der auch vor einigen Monaten aus Pakistan floh. Die beiden kommen aus zwei weit voneinander entfernten Gebieten Pakistans, aber sie sprechen die gleiche Sprache und sie lieben die pakistanische Küche, das verbindet ungemein. „Früher habe ich nie gekocht, das hat meine Mutter gemacht. Aber zum Glück habe ich gut aufgepasst, denn jetzt muss ich das alles selbst tun.“ Sein Lieblingsgericht „Keema Matar“ kocht er immer wieder gerne – mir hat es unheimlich gut geschmeckt!

Caro, Sulemans Kochpartnerin

A little more than one year ago, Suleman came from Pakistan (Islamabad) to Germany. Since then he has been living in an asylum home in Marienfelde that is located in the outskirts of Berlin. Suleman loves the German capital Berlin. “Berlin is so colourful and in addition to that not so expensive. I would love to stay here”, he explains with a big smile on his face. Beforehand, Suleman lived two years in London with his sister but he never really liked it. “It's expensive, crowded and offers little opportunity to live a good life.”

Here in Germany the 29 year old Suleman is sharing a room with a nice Pakistani and he already won many friends who share a similar fate. When we met for cooking, Suleman arrived with his friend Mohammed who also flew from Pakistan a few months ago. Even though they come from different regions they speak the same language and share their love for the Pakistani cuisine. This connects immensely. “I never used to cook – my mother always did it. But luckily I paid attention because now I have to do all by myself.” Suleman cooks his most favourite dish “Keema Matar” frequently and I enjoyed it a lot!

Caro, Suleman's cooking partner

HUMMUS

FATMA

10

HUMMUS

SYRIEN · SYRIA

1 Dose Kichererbsen
1 can of chickpeas

Saft von 2 Zitronen
juice of 2 lemons

207
3 EL Tahina
3 tbsp tahina

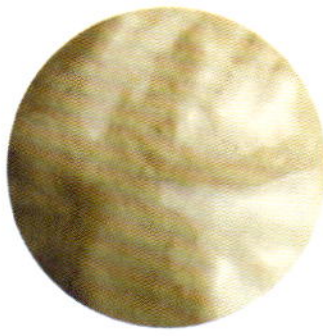

2 – 3 Knoblauchzehen
2 – 3 cloves of garlic

206
Pul Biber
pul biber

Kreuzkümmel
cumin

Olivenöl
olive oil

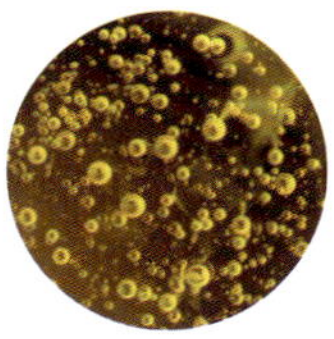

Salz
salt

dieses Gericht ist vegan
this dish is vegan

KICHERERBSENPASTE
CHICKPEA PASTE

- Zuerst den Knoblauch in kleine Stücke schneiden und zerdrücken.
- Dann die Kichererbsen abseihen und einige zurückbehalten.
- Die übrigen Kichererbsen mit etwas Flüssigkeit aus der Dose, der Tahina, dem Zitronensaft, dem zerdrückten Knoblauch und Salz fein pürieren.
- Auf einem Teller verteilen und mit den restlichen Kichererbsen verzieren.
- Vor dem Essen den Hummus mit etwas Öl beträufeln und mit Pul Biber und Kreuzkümmel bestreuen.

- Finely chop the garlic and then crush.
- Strain the chickpeas and reserve a few for decoration.
- Blend the chickpeas with some liquid from the can as well as the tahina, lemon juice, garlic, and salt until you have a smooth puree.
- Serve on a large plate and decorate with the remaining chickpeas.
- Sprinkle some cumin and pul biber, then drizzle with a little olive oil before serving.

FATMA

Fatma kam im Oktober 2013 mit ihrem Mann und ihren zwei Kindern aus Syrien nach Deutschland. Hier lebt sie in einem Asylbewerberheim in Ebenhausen in Unterfranken. Eines von Fatmas Hobbys ist Kochen. Am liebsten mag sie das selbstgemachte Hummus, da es sie immer an ihre Heimat Homs erinnert, wo es für sie einfach das beste Hummus in Syrien gibt. Beim Kochen hört sie oft arabische Musik.

Fatma lebte sehr gerne in Syrien. Sie schätzt das gute Miteinander und friedliche Zusammenleben vieler ethnischer Gruppen wie Christen, Kurden, Syrer und Palästinenser in ihrer Heimat sehr. Dieses zeige sich auch jetzt im Asylbewerberheim, wo Menschen dieser Gruppen aufeinandertreffen und auf engstem Raum zusammenleben, erzählt sie.

Trotzdem gibt es auch vieles, was sie an Deutschland schon zu schätzen gelernt hat. Zum Beispiel die soziale Gerechtigkeit – hier werden auch ärmere Menschen auf Ämtern oder Behörden gut behandelt. In Syrien dagegen läuft es oft über Bestechungsgelder, die viele Menschen nicht zahlen können. Auch neu für Fatma ist das gleichberechtigte Zusammenleben von Mann und Frau, wie wir es in Deutschland gewohnt sind, denn das ist in Syrien nicht in allen Familien üblich.

Conny, Fatmas Kochpartnerin

Fatma came to Germany from Syria in October 2013 with her husband and two children. They live together in a refugee home in Ebenhausen, Unterfranken.

One of Fatma's hobbies is cooking. She likes making homemade hummus because it always reminds her of her hometown Homs, where you can find the best hummus in all of Syria. Fatma often listens to Arabic music whilst cooking.

Fatma felt happy living in Syria – in her homeland she could appreciate the togetherness and peaceful coexistence of many ethnic groups such as Christians, Kurds, Syrians and Palestinians. She tells me that this is also true for the refugee home where people from these groups meet and live together in a confined space.

But there are many things she has learned to appreciate here in Germany, too. For example, the social justice system here means that poorer people are treated better in offices and agencies whereas in Syria, bribery is commonplace and means that many people cannot afford services. What is also new for Fatma is the equal coexistence of men and women that we are accustomed to in Germany. This is not typical for all families in Syria.

Conny, Fatma's cooking partner

DAMBOU

MOUHAMED

80

DAMBOU

NIGER

½ rote Paprika
½ red pepper

250 g Schwarzaugenbohnen
250 g black-eyed beans
207

½ Strauch Mangold
½ shrub chard

2 Karotten
2 carrots

½ Fenchelknolle
½ fennel bulb

1 kl. Zwiebel, 2 Knoblauchzehen
1 small onion, 2 cloves of garlic

2 Tomaten
2 tomatoes

4 – 6 Samen vom Johannisbrotbaum
4 – 6 seeds from the carob tree
205

1 rote Chilischote
1 red chili

100 – 150 g Tomatenmark
100 – 150 g tomato paste

206
150 ml Palmöl
150 ml palm oil

Salz, 1 Brühwürfel
salt, 1 stock cube

dieses Gericht ist vegan
this dish is vegan

SCHWARZAUGENBOHNENEINTOPF MIT JOHANNISBROTBAUMSAMEN

BLACK-EYED BEAN STEW WITH CAROB SEEDS

- Die Bohnen in 1 l Wasser aufkochen und 20 min kochen lassen.
- In der Zwischenzeit den Mangold, die Möhren, den Fenchel und die Paprika in kleine Teile schneiden, die Zwiebeln grob und die Chilischoten fein hacken.
- Das Bohnenwasser abgießen, die Bohnen kurz abwaschen und den Topf mit frischem Wasser auffüllen. Das Wasser erneut zum Kochen bringen.
- Tomatenmark unter die Bohnen rühren, Brühwürfel hinzugeben.
- Das gesamte Gemüse und die gehackten Chilischoten in den Topf geben und weitere 20 min kochen lassen.
- Palmöl hinzugeben und mit Salz abschmecken.
- Knoblauch und Johannisbrotbaumsamen in einem Mörser gründlich zermahlen und anschließend zum Eintopf geben.
- Mit Brot oder Fufu (204) servieren.

- Cook the beans in 1 l of water for 20 min.
- In the meantime, cut the chard, fennel, carrots, and the pepper, chop the onion and finely chop the chili.
- Pour off the water from the beans and wash, refill the cooking pot with fresh water and cook again.
- Add tomato paste and the stock cube, stir everything well.
- Add the vegetables and the chili and cook for 20 min more.
- Add palm oil and season with salt.
- Grind the garlic and the seeds of the carob tree in a mortar and add it to the stew.
- Serve with bread or Fufu (204).

BRING ZEIT MIT, IN AFRIKA DAUERT ES LANGE EIN GERICHT ZUZUBEREITEN.

Mouhamed

BRING ENOUGH TIME, IN AFRICA IT TAKES A LONG TIME TO PREPARE A DISH.

Mouhamed

MOUHAMED

Als Mouhamed und ich uns zum Kochen verabredeten, sagte er: „Bring Zeit mit, in Afrika dauert es lange ein Gericht zuzubereiten." Tatsächlich standen wir mehrere Stunden in der Küche, aber es ist unheimlich schön das Kochen mit Gemütlichkeit und Ruhe zu verbinden. Dann schmeckt am Ende alles doppelt so gut und es bleibt viel Zeit für interessante Gespräche.
Mouhamed lebt seit etwas mehr als einem Jahr in Deutschland. Ursprünglich kommt er aus Niger, wo er zusammen mit seinen zwölf Geschwistern – elf Jungen und nur einem Mädchen – aufwuchs. Mouhamed spricht insgesamt neun Sprachen. Bevor er nach Deutschland kam, studierte er Philosophie und Literatur bis zum Diplomabschluss.
Der junge Mann kochte schon immer gern. Die Küche ist für ihn der Ort, an dem die Familie zusammenkommt, um der Mutter beim Kochen zu helfen und natürlich um gemeinsam zu essen. „Kochen ist in Afrika eine sehr wichtige Fähigkeit. Denn wenn du nicht kochen kannst, kannst du nicht verheiratet werden", erklärt Mouhamed lachend. Dementsprechend gut schmeckt auch sein Gemüseeintopf Dambou.

Gerrit, Mouhameds Kochpartner

When Mouhamed and I met for cooking, he told me: "Bring enough time, in Africa it takes a long time to prepare a dish." We spent several hours in the kitchen but it was actually incredibly nice to combine cooking with comfort and peace. In the end, everything tasted twice as good and there was plenty of time for interesting conversations.
Mouhamed has been living in Germany for a little more than one year. Originally he is from Niger where he grew up together with his twelve siblings – eleven brothers and only one sister! Mouhamed can speak nine languages and before he came to Germany, he studied philosophy and literature.
Mouhamed always liked to cook. The kitchen is the place where the family comes together in order to help the mother cooking and, of course, to eat together. "Cooking is a very important skill in Africa. Because if you cannot cook, you cannot marry", he explains, laughing. It is no surprise then that Mouhamed's vegetable stew Dambou tastes exceptionally good.

Gerrit, Mouhamed's cooking partner

9

PLOW
DOLMA

AYSUN

75

PLOW

ASERBAIDSCHAN · AZERBAIJAN

500 g Kalbs- oder Rindergulasch
500 g stewing beef or veal

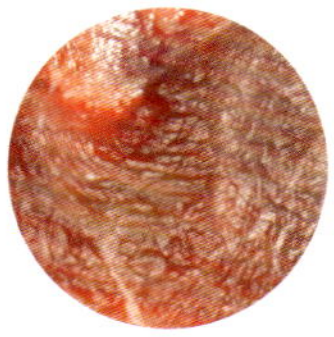

800 g Basmatireis
800 g basmati rice

4–5 Zwiebeln
4–5 onions

200 g Maronen
200 g chestnuts

100 g gelbe Rosinen
100 g yellow raisins

100 g getrocknete gelbe Pflaumen
100 g dried yellow plums

100 g getrocknete Aprikosen
100 g dried apricots

2 Eier
2 eggs

2 EL türkischer Joghurt (10%)
2 tbsp Turkish yoghurt (10%)

2 TL Safranfäden
2 tsp saffron threads

Saft von ½ Zitrone
juice of ½ lemon

Kurkuma, Salz, Pfeffer, 50 g Butter, Olivenöl
curcuma, salt, pepper, 50 g butter, olive oil

statt Rinderhack Sojafleisch, statt Butter Pflanzenmargarine verwenden
use soya meat instead of minced beaf; vegetable margarine instead of butter

BUNTE REISPFANNE

COLOURFUL RICE DISH

- Reis waschen, mit 1½ EL Salz in 2 l Wasser 15 min einweichen, dann 15 min kochen. Trockenobst in Wasser einweichen.
- Fleisch 45 min in ungesalzenem Wasser kochen. Dann die Fleischbrühe auffangen, Fleisch beiseitestellen.
- Bei den Maronen das obere Ende abschneiden. 15 min in der Brühe kochen.
- Zwiebeln in dünne Ringe schneiden. Safran in ein Schälchen geben und mit kochendem Wasser übergießen.
- Zwiebeln in einer Pfanne in Olivenöl glasig dünsten. Fleisch zugeben, salzen und pfeffern, unter ständigem Wenden braten, bis das Fleisch gut durch ist.
- Maronen nach Ende der Kochzeit schälen und zum Fleisch geben. Trockenobst abtropfen lassen und ebenfalls zugeben. Zitronensaft mit 3 EL Wasser und 1 TL Kurkuma verrühren und über das Fleisch geben.
- In einer Schale Joghurt und Eier mit 3 EL gekochtem Reis verrühren. Butter in einem großen Topf zerlassen, Joghurtmischung zugeben, gleichmäßig verteilen und stocken lassen. Den Reis auf die Joghurtmischung geben und darauf verteilen (nicht verrühren).
- Safran sowie Kurkuma und etwas Olivenöl über den Reis geben, vorsichtig unterheben. Ein Geschirrtuch über den Topf legen, den Deckel auflegen und den Reis so weitere 30 min garen.
- Reis auf einer großen Platte anrichten. Trockenobst und Maronen darauf, Fleisch rundherum verteilen. Die Joghurtmischung vom Boden des Topfes lösen, in Streifen schneiden und dekorativ auf der Platte anordnen.

- Wash the rice, add 1½ tbsp salt, soak for 15 min in 2 l of water, then cook for 15 min. Soak the dried fruits.
- Cook the meat for 45 min in unsalted water. Then strain and reserve the broth and set the meat aside.
- Cut the end off of the chestnuts and cook for 15 min in the broth.
- Cut the onions into thin rings. Put the saffron threads into a bowl and pour over a little boiling water.
- Heat olive oil, fry the onions, add the meat, and fry whilst stirring. Season with salt and pepper.
- Peel the chestnuts and add to the meat. Add the dried fruits. Mix the lemon juice with 3 tbsp water and 1 tsp curcuma. Add it to the meat.
- Mix yoghurt, eggs, and 3 tbsp cooked rice in a bowl. Melt butter in a cooking pot, add the yoghurt mixture, and let it thicken. Add the rest of the rice to the yoghurt mixture (do not mix).
- Fold in saffron, curcuma and olive oil. Put a tea towel on top of the pot, cover with the lid and let the rice cook for 30 min.
- Serve the rice on a big platter, decorate with the dried fruits and the chestnuts and spread the meat around it. Remove the baked yoghurt mixture from the cooking pot, cut into small strips and arrange neatly on the platter.

60

DOLMA

ASERBAIDSCHAN · AZERBAIJAN

500 g Rinderhack
500 g minced beef

4 Zwiebeln
4 onions

½ Bund frischer Dill
½ bunch of fresh dill

½ Bund frische Minze
½ bunch of fresh mint

100 g Rundkornreis
100 g long grain rice

1 Glas Weinblätter
1 jar of vine leaves

250 g Butter
250 g butter

Salz, Pfeffer, Olivenöl
salt, pepper, olive oil

- Minze und Dill fein hacken. Die Zwiebel ebenfalls fein hacken, danach mit Küchenpapier trocken tupfen. (Es soll keine Zwiebelflüssigkeit dabei sein.) Den Reis 15 min in Wasser einweichen.
- In einer Schüssel das Hackfleisch, die Zwiebeln, den Dill, die Minze, die Butter und den Reis gut miteinander vermischen, salzen und pfeffern. Etwas Olivenöl zugeben und zu einem geschmeidigen Teig verarbeiten.
- Die Weinblätter 15 min in ca. 1½ l Wasser kochen, anschließend die Stiele entfernen. Auf die Hälfte des Weinblatts eine daumengroße Menge der Hackfleischmischung geben und das Blatt quadratisch so falten, dass sich das Ganze nicht wieder auflöst. So mit ¾ der Weinblätter verfahren, den Rest aufheben.
- Den Boden eines großen Topfes mit den restlichen Weinblättern bedecken, dann die gefüllten Weinblätter darauflegen. Mit ca. 400 ml Wasser bei geschlossenem Deckel bei großer Hitze 30 min garen.

Gefüllte Weinblätter
Stuffed Vine Leaves

- Finely chop the dill and the mint. Chop the onions into small pieces and blot dry with paper towel. (All the liquid from the onions should be soaked up.) Soak the rice for 15 min.
- Mix the minced beef, onions, dill, mint, butter and rice together and season with salt and pepper. Add some olive oil and work into a smooth dough.
- Cook the vine leaves for approximately 15 min in 1½ l water. Remove the stems and place a small amount of the minced meat mixture on one half of the leaf; fold into a small rectangle. Repeat this with ¾ of the vine leaves.
- Cover the bottom of a pan with the remaining vine leaves and place the filled vine leaves on top. Add approximately 400 ml water and cook for 30 min on high with the lid closed.

Es ist jetzt fast ein Jahr her, dass die 46-jährige Aysun aus Baku, Aserbaidschan, zusammen mit ihrem Mann nach Deutschland kam. Nach einem kurzen Aufenthalt in Schöppingen ging es für sie weiter nach Bochum.
Bevor die beiden nach Deutschland kamen, lebten sie sieben Jahre lang in Moskau. Da ihr kranker Mann in Russland nicht adäquat behandelt werden konnte, beschlossen die beiden nach Deutschland zu gehen. Hier fühlen sie sich mittlerweile sehr wohl und sind sehr zufrieden mit der medizinischen Versorgung. Aysun möchte so schnell wie möglich besser Deutsch lernen, am besten durch Kontakte zu Deutschen. Danach hofft sie, sich irgendwann ihren größten Wunsch erfüllen zu können: einen Führerschein zu machen und flexibler zu sein.
Eines ihrer Lieblingsgerichte ist Plow. Das ist ein typisches Nationalgericht aus Aserbaidschan. Es gibt viele verschiedene Möglichkeiten Plow zuzubereiten, aber es basiert immer auf Reis und Fleisch und wird normalerweise mit Gemüse, getrockneten Früchten oder Nüssen serviert. Plow wird auch oft für große Feiern zubereitet.

Claudia, Aysuns Kochpartnerin

Aysun is 46 years old and comes from Baku, Azerbaijan. She came to Germany with her husband just under a year ago. They were initially based in Schöppingen before moving to Bochum.
Before the couple moved to Germany they spent seven years living in Moscow. However, Aysun's husband was unwell and did not have access to adequate healthcare. It was due to this that they decided to come to Germany. Here, they feel happy and are very satisfied with the medical care available to them. Aysun wants to improve her German as quickly as possible, preferably through contact with German people. After improving her German, Aysun hopes to achieve her biggest ambition: to get a driver's license and have more flexibility.
One of her favourite dishes is Plow. It is one of the national dishes of Azerbaijan. There are many different ways to prepare the dish. However, the dish is always based on rice and meat and is usually served with vegetables, dried fruits or nuts. Plow is often prepared for large celebrations.

Claudia, Aysun's cooking partner

OOZIE

WAEL

90

OOZIE

SYRIEN · SYRIA

1 Tasse Basmatireis
1 cup of basmati rice

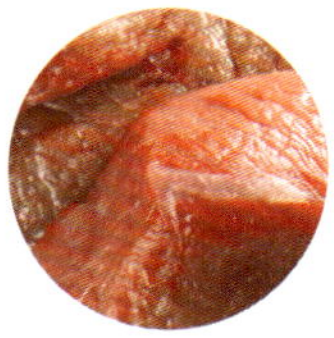

150 g Rindfleisch
150 g beef

250 g TK-Erbsen
250 g frozen peas

250 g Yufka-Teig
250 g yufka dough 207

75 g ganze Mandeln
75 g whole almonds

40 g Pinienkerne
40 g pine nuts

100 g Butter
100 g butter

1 EL Baharat
1 tbsp baharat 203

Salz, Pfeffer, Pflanzenöl
salt, pepper, vegetable oil

statt Rindfleisch Seitan, statt Butter Pflanzenmagarine verwenden
use seitan instead of beef; vegetable magarine instead of butter

Gefüllte Yufka-Teigtaschen

Stuffed Yufka Turnovers

- Den Reis für ca. 30 min in Wasser einweichen.
- Das Fleisch in kleine Stücke schneiden und in einem Topf in Öl und 1 EL Butter anbraten. Anschließend die Erbsen zugeben, nach 5 min ständigen Rührens 2 Tassen kochendes Wasser hinzufügen und 5 min köcheln lassen.
- Währenddessen die Mandeln mit kochendem Wasser übergießen und schälen, dann halbieren. Anschließend zusammen mit den Pinienkernen in einer trockenen Pfanne kurz anrösten.
- Den Reis abgießen und zum Erbsen-Fleisch-Gemisch hinzufügen. 75 g Butter hinzugeben und mit Baharat, Salz und Pfeffer würzen. Köcheln lassen, bis der Reis gar ist. Vom Herd nehmen und die Mandeln und Pinienkerne unterrühren.
- Den Ofen auf 200° vorheizen. 2 Blätter des Yufka-Teigs übereinanderlegen, mit einem kleinen Teil der Masse füllen, zu einer Kugel formen und verschließen. Währenddessen die restliche Butter schmelzen.
- Die Teigkugeln in eine eingefettete Backform legen und mit flüssiger Butter bestreichen. So auch mit der übrigen Masse verfahren und 30 min im vorgeheizten Ofen backen, bis die Oozis goldbraun sind.

Dazu passt Tzatziki.

- Soak the rice for 30 min.
- Cut the beef into cubes and fry in a pot with the oil and 1 tbsp butter. Add the peas and stir continually for 5 min. Then add 2 cups of boiling water and allow to simmer for an additional 5 min.
- Meanwhile, pour boiling water over the almonds, then peel and cut in half. Toast the almonds and pine nuts in a dry pan.
- Time to drain the rice and add to the peas-and-meat mixture! Leave to simmer until the rice is cooked. Melt 75 g butter with the baharat and season with salt and pepper. Remove the pot from the heat and stir in the almonds and pine nuts.
- Place 2 sheets of dough on top of one another, spoon a little bit of the rice mixture into the centre, shape into a ball and then seal the edges to create a parcel. Melt the remaining butter.
- Place the parcels onto a greased baking pan and brush with melted butter. Repeat with the remaining mixture. Bake in a preheated oven at 200° for approximately 30 min, until the Oozies are golden brown.

Tzatziki works well as a side dish.

WAEL

Wael ist 33 Jahre alt und kommt aus Damaskus, Syrien. Dort arbeitete er als Übersetzer und persönlicher Assistent in der US-Botschaft. Diese Karriere und sein ganzes Leben dort musste er im März 2013 bei seiner Flucht über den Libanon, die Türkei und Rumänien nach Deutschland hinter sich lassen, da seine Arbeit und seine Mithilfe in einer Hilfsorganisation ihn in sehr große politische Schwierigkeiten mit dem Assad-Regime gebracht hatten.
Nun lebt er im Großraum München, besucht einen Deutschkurs und arbeitet nebenher ehrenamtlich als Übersetzer im Jugendsozialwerk.
Er träumt davon hier in Deutschland seine Karriere – vielleicht sogar wieder in der US-Botschaft – fortsetzen zu können und irgendwann eine Familie zu gründen.
Kochen lernte er erst hier in Deutschland durch viel Ausprobieren und die Kommunikation mit seinen Schwestern und seiner Mutter über Skype. Mittlerweile hat er aber schon eine ziemliche Bandbreite an Rezepten erlernt und einige sogar selbst kreiert.

Rebekka, Waels Kochpartnerin

Wael is 33 years old and originates from Damascus. He used to work in the American Embassy in Syria as a translator and personal assistant. Due to the nature of his work and his engagement with aid groups, Wael encountered political difficulties related to the Assad regime. It was because of this that Wael had to leave behind his entire life and career. He fled from Syria to Germany in March 2013 via Lebanon, Turkey and Romania.
At the moment Wael lives in Greater Munich, participates in a German course and also works voluntarily as a translator for a social youth project. He dreams about rebuilding his career in Germany – maybe even aiming for a position in the US Embassy. In the future he would like to have a family of his own.
It was in Germany that Wael discovered his passion for cooking. His creativity in the kitchen began with trial and error, but developed through frequent discussions with his sisters and mother over Skype.

Rebekka, Wael's cooking partner

I PREFER TO USE SPICES THAT MAKE MY KITCHEN SMELL LIKE MY OLD HOME.

Wael

über den TELLERRAND kochen
UNTERSTÜTZE UNS
...und werde Fördermitglied!
FLÜCHTLINGE & EINHEIMISCHE ZUSAMMEN BRINGEN
UEBERDENTELLERRANDKOCHEN.DE • FÜR EIN BESSERES WIR

GEMEINSAM FÜR EIN BESSERES WIR

Du möchtest Fördermitglied werden? Wunderbar!
Fülle einfache dieses Formular aus und sende es an:

Über den Tellerrand kochen e.V.
c/o social impact lab
Muskauer Straße 24
10997 Berlin

JA ich möchte Fördermitglied werden,
mit einem Monatsbeitrag von:

- ◯ 5€
- ◯ 25€
- ◯ 50€
- ◯ ____ individueller Beitrag (Minimum 5€)

Meine Kontaktdaten

Vor -und Nachname* ____________________

Straße und Hausnummer* ____________________

PLZ und Ort* ____________________

E-Mail Adresse* ____________________

Telefon (gern mobil) ____________________

* Erforderliche Angaben
Hab keine Angst vor ungewünschter Werbung! Wir nutzen deine Daten selbstverständlich nur zu Zwecken der Mitgliederverwaltung und wir geben deine Daten nicht an Dritte weiter.

Kontoinhaber ____________________

IBAN ____________________

BIC ____________________

Kreditinstitut ____________________

Ich ermächtige Über den Tellerrand kochen e.V., Zahlungen von meinem Konto mittels Lastschrift zum 15. des Folgemonats vom Antragsdatum einzuziehen.
Zugleich weise ich mein Kreditinstitut an, die von Über den Tellerrand kochen e.V. auf mein Konto gezogenen Lastschriften einzulösen. Hinweis: Ich kann innerhalb von acht Wochen, beginnend mit dem Belastungsdatum, die Erstattung des belasteten Betrages verlangen. Es gelten dabei die mit meinem Kreditinstitut vereinbarten Bedingungen.

Ort, Datum, Unterschrift ____________________

FRAGEN? rafael@ueberdentellerrandkochen.de 0152 - 56145986

ICH BENUTZE AM LIEBSTEN GEWÜRZE, DIE MEINE KÜCHE SO RIECHEN LASSEN WIE DIE IN MEINEM ALTEN HAUS.

Wael

OGBONO SOUP

ABIOLA

150 - 180

OGBONO SOUP

NIGERIA

500 g Ziegenfleisch ohne Knochen

500 g goat meat without bones

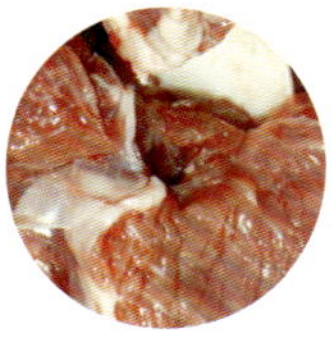

1 rote Zwiebel

1 red onion

1 Brühwürfel

1 stock cube

2 getrocknete Sardinen

2 dried sardines

205

1 Paket Ogbono

1 packet ogbono

1 kl. Tüte getrocknete Flusskrebse

1 small bag of dried crayfish

2 Hände voll Spinat, gewaschen und gehackt

2 handfuls of spinach, washed and chopped

500 g Yamsmehl

500 g yam flour

207

206

250 ml Palmöl

250 ml palm oil

2 gehäufte TL gemahlener Pfeffer

2 heaped tsp ground pepper

WESTAFRIKANISCHE FISCHSUPPE MIT GETROCKNETEN MANGOKERNEN
WEST AFRICAN FISH SOUP WITH DRIED MANGO SEEDS

- Das Ziegenfleisch zerkleinern und mit einer gewürfelten roten Zwiebel und einem Brühwürfel in leicht gesalzenem Wasser ca. 2 h kochen, bis das Fleisch gar ist. Das Wasser sollte das Fleisch bedecken.
- Die Sardinen waschen, grob zerkleinern und in leicht gesalzenem Wasser ca. 20 min garen.
- Ogbono (getrocknete Mangokerne) fein hacken, mit dem Palmöl verrühren und zum gekochten Ziegenfleisch geben.
- Die getrockneten Flusskrebse sehr fein hacken und zusammen mit den gekochten Sardinen, dem gemahlenen Pfeffer und dem Spinat ebenfalls zum Ziegenfleisch geben und alles unterrühren. Das Ganze ca. 10 – 15 min kochen lassen.
- Für das Pounded Yam ca. ¾ l Wasser mit 1 TL Öl zum Kochen bringen und so viel Yamsmehl einrühren, bis sich ein Kloß bildet.
- Den Kloß im Topf leicht abbrennen lassen und zusammen mit der Ogbono-Suppe auf einem tiefen Teller servieren.

- Chop the red onion and goat meat into pieces and boil for approximately 2 h in lightly salted water along with a stock cube. Cook until the meat is done (juices run clear). The water should cover the meat.
- Wash the sardines, chop into pieces and simmer in slightly salted water until cooked, approximately 20 min.
- Finely chop the ogbono (dried mango seeds), mix with palm oil, and add to the cooked goat meat.
- Finely chop the crayfish, combine with the ground pepper and spinach; add this mixture and the fish to the goat meat and stir whilst simmering, approximately 10 – 15 min.
- For the Pounded Yam boil ¾ l water and 1 tbsp oil together, then add yam flour until a lump begins to form.
- Allow the yam flour dumpling to burn slightly in the pot and serve it with the ogbono soup.

ABIOLA

Letzte Woche habe ich meinen Freund Abiola zum gemeinsamen Kochen eingeladen. Abiola brachte noch seinen Freund Maik mit und es gab etwas typisch Nigerianisches: Ogbono Soup und Pounded Yam. Wir hatten an diesem Abend viel Spaß zusammen.
Als im Herbst des letzten Jahres immer mehr Lampedusa-Flüchtlinge nach Hamburg kamen und die Stadt Probleme mit der Unterbringung hatte, hat sich meine Gemeinde spontan dazu entschlossen den Jugendkeller des Gemeindehauses in eine Notunterkunft umzufunktionieren. Es war ein Winternotprogramm für Flüchtlinge, das, in Anlehnung an das Winternotprogramm der Stadt Hamburg für Obdachlose, Bedürftigen in der Zeit von November bis April Obhut bietet.
Ich war als ehrenamtlicher Betreuer in diesem Programm tätig und Abiola war der erste Teilnehmer. Das Winternotprogramm ist längst beendet und aus Flüchtling und Betreuer sind Freunde geworden.
Als ich Abiola kennenlernte, besaß er nur die Kleidung, die er am Leib trug, etwas Kleidung zum Wechseln und eine kleine Umhängetasche mit ein paar persönlichen Gegenständen und dennoch habe ich ihm viel zu verdanken, denn er hat mich an etwas erinnert, was ich fast vergessen hätte und für mich schon selbstverständlich wurde. Jeden Morgen, nachdem ich Abiola geweckt hatte, hat er gebetet: „Herr, danke, dass ich lebe."

Helmut, Abiolas Kochpartner

Last week I invited my friend Abiola for dinner. Abiola brought his friend Maik and we cooked something typically Nigerian: Ogbono Soup and Pounded Yam. We had a lot of fun together that evening.
In autumn last year, when many Lampedusa refugees arrived in Hamburg and the city had problems regarding their accommodation, our community spontaneously decided to convert the youth cellar into emergency accommodation. Together with Hamburg's winter emergency program we took care and provided shelter for refugees and other people in need during the period from November until April.
I worked there as a volunteer and Abiola was our first participant. The whole winter emergency program is long over, however the volunteers and refugees built up strong relationships that still last.
When I first met Abiola, he owned only the clothes he was wearing, some things to change and a small bag with a few personal belongings. And yet, I am so thankful that he reminded me of something that I had almost forgotten in between my daily routines. Every morning after I awoke Abiola, he prayed: "Lord, thank you that I'm alive."

Helmut, Abiola's cooking partner

EATING IS PART OF EVERY CULTURE AND I AM ALWAYS CURIOUS TO GET TO KNOW NEW CULTURES.

Helmut

ESSEN IST TEIL JEDER KULTUR UND ICH BIN IMMER WIEDER NEUGIERIG, NEUE KULTUREN KENNENZULERNEN

SAFIULLAH

BIRYANI

40

BIRYANI

PAKISTAN

500 g Hähnchenschenkel

500 g chicken drumsticks

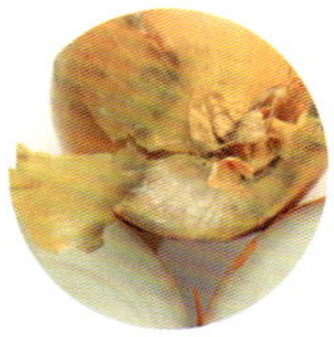

5 kl. Zwiebeln

5 small onions

500 g Basmatireis

500 g basmati rice

10 g Granatapfelkerne

10 g pomegranate seeds

50 g Naturjoghurt

50 g natural yoghurt

getrocknete Nelken
(ca. 5 Stück)

dried cloves
(approx. 5 pieces)

203

2 EL Bombay Biryani

2 tbsp Bombay Biryani

ca. 8 Lorbeerblätter

approx. 8 bay leaves

204

2 EL Garam Masala

2 tbsp garam masala

Salz, schwarzer Pfeffer,
Paprikapulver (scharf), Pflanzenöl

salt, black pepper,
spicy paprika powder, vegetable oil

Würzige Reispfanne mit Granatapfelkernen
Spicy Rice with Pomegranate Seeds

- Die Zwiebeln in grobe Stücke hacken.
- Pflanzenöl in einem großen Kochtopf erhitzen.
- Das Fett am Knochen der Hähnchenschenkel mit einem scharfen Messer abtrennen. Anschließend unter kaltem Wasser abwaschen, abtropfen lassen und beiseitestellen.
- Zwiebeln im Kochtopf scharf anbraten.
- Den Reis unter kaltem Wasser abwaschen und, wenn möglich, in einem Reiskocher kochen.
- Lorbeerblätter in der Hand zerkleinern und mit Salz, Pfeffer, Garam Masala und Paprikapulver zu den Zwiebeln in den Topf geben.
- ¼ Glas Wasser hinzufügen, kurz umrühren.
- Die Hähnchenschenkel zur Zwiebel-Gewürzmischung hinzugeben und auf mittlerer Hitze rundherum darin anbraten.
- 1 EL der Bombay Biryani-Gewürzmischung hinzugeben und unter ständigem Rühren ca. 20 – 25 min braten.
- 1 Glas Wasser hinzugeben, die Hitze reduzieren und mit geschlossenem Deckel weiterkochen lassen.
- Den Reis und das Fleisch in einer großen Schüssel anrichten.
- Den Joghurt in einer extra Schüssel mit 1 EL der Bombay Biryani-Gewürzmischung vermengen und zusammen servieren. Die Granatapfelkerne darauf verteilen.

- Chop the onions into coarse pieces.
- Heat vegetable oil in a large cooking pot.
- With a sharp knife, trim the fat from the chicken thighs. Rinse the chicken with cold water and set aside.
- Sear the onions in the oil.
- Wash the rice with cold water and cook as per the instructions (if possible with a rice cooker).
- Grind the bay leaves and add to the fried onions along with the salt, pepper, garam masala, and paprika powder.
- Add ¼ glass of water and stir briefly.
- Add the chicken drumsticks to the spicy onion mixture and fry on medium.
- Then add 1 tbsp Bombay Biryani spice mixture and fry for approximately 20 – 25 min, stirring constantly.
- Add 1 glass of water, reduce the heat and simmer with the lid on.
- Arrange the rice and meat in a large bowl.
- Combine the yoghurt with 1 tbsp spice mixture and serve with the rice and meat, sprinkle pomegranate seeds on top for the finishing touch.

SAFIULLAH

Safiullah ist 18 Jahre alt und kommt aus der Region Punjab in Pakistan. Seit fast zwei Jahren lebt er nun in Deutschland. Anfang 2013 zog er in die Wohngemeinschaft der *outback-stiftung*. Derzeit besucht er die 9. Klasse eines Berufskollegs. Er hofft irgendwann eine Ausbildung beginnen zu können, so wie sein Mitbewohner Abdoulaye.
Das Gericht kennt Safiullah noch aus seiner Heimat Pakistan. Biryani isst er ganz besonders gern, in seiner Heimat aß er es oft mit seiner Familie. Mindestens zwei bis drei Mal pro Woche wurde es daheim gekocht. Dort wurde es allerdings meistens mit Ziegenfleisch zubereitet. Selbst kochen musste er zuhause jedoch nicht. Seine Familie beschäftigte eine Haushälterin. Nun übt er fleißig, um auch selbst seine pakistanischen Leibgerichte zubereiten zu können. Manchmal fällt ihm das noch schwer. Sein Bezugsbetreuer Milan unterstützt ihn dabei, so gut es geht. Am liebsten gehen die beiden allerdings zusammen Pizza essen.
In der pakistanischen Küche wird viel Salz verwendet. Davon gibt es in Safiullahs Heimat sehr viel für wenig Geld. Während des Kochens serviert Safiullah eine saftige Wassermelone – jedes Stück wird vor dem Verzehr gründlich gesalzen. Zum Essen versammelt man sich gemeinsam am Tisch, das Essen wird in einer großen Schüssel serviert und jeder nimmt sich so viel, wie er möchte. Später am Abend gibt es dann ein Glas heiße Milch vor dem Einschlafen. Im Sommer werden die sehr warmen Nächte draußen oder auf den Dächern der Häuser verbracht. So lässt es sich angenehm schlafen.

Milan, Safiullahs Kochpartner

Safiullah is 18 years old and comes from the Punjab, a region in Pakistan. He has been living in Germany for nearly two years and in 2013 he moved into a room at a residential community of the *outback foundation*. At the moment Safiullah is in the 9th grade of a vocational college. He hopes to start an apprenticeship like his flatmate very soon. Safiullah knows the dish Biryani from his home in Pakistan. He loves Biryani and used to eat it at least two to three times per week with his family – back home the dish is usually cooked with goat meat. When Safiullah lived in Pakistan he did not have to cook as his family had a housekeeper. Nowadays he practices diligently so that he can prepare his favourite Pakistani dishes by himself. It is not always easy, but his care supervisor Milan supports him as best as he can. Mughlai cuisine uses a great deal of salt, in Pakistan you can buy salt cheaply in bulk. Even a piece of a juicy melon is thoroughly salted before eating!
At dinnertime, everyone gathers around the table. A big bowl is placed in the middle and everyone takes as much as they want. Later in the evening, a glass of hot milk is served before everyone goes to bed. The warm nights in summer are usually spent outside or on the roofs of houses where everyone can sleep comfortably.

Milan, Safiullah's cooking partner

MA'ALOOBE
FASOOLYE BZEIT

120

MA'ALOOBE

SYRIEN · SYRIA

250 g Basmatireis
250 g basmati rice

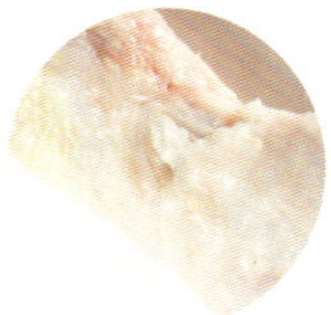

700 g Hühnerfleisch mit Knochen
700 g chicken on the bone

300 g Auberginen, in Scheiben
300 g aubergines, sliced

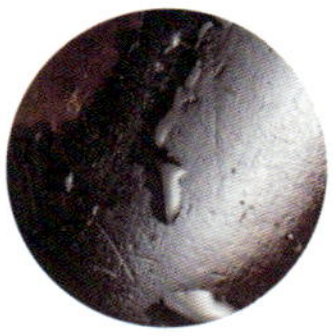

300 g Kartoffeln, in Scheiben
300 g potatoes, sliced

1 gr. Zwiebel, halbiert
1 large onion, halved

Saft von 1 Zitrone
juice of 1 lemon

1 Zimtstange
1 cinnamon stick

4 Kardamomkapseln
4 cardamom pods

206

Öl zum Frittieren
oil for deep-frying

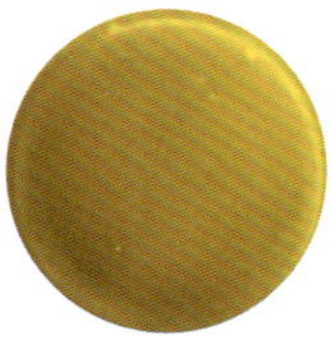

Salz, Pfeffer, Olivenöl
salt, pepper, olive oil

REIS-GEMÜSE-SCHICHTEN MIT HÜHNCHENFLEISCH

LAYERS OF RICE AND VEGETABLES TOPPED WITH CHICKEN

- Zunächst das Hühnerfleisch mit Wasser waschen, mit Salz und Zitronensaft einreiben und 5 min stehen lassen. Anschließend das Fleisch erneut mit Wasser abspülen, trocken tupfen und für 15 – 20 min bei starker Hitze in einem großen Topf in Wasser aufkochen lassen, dann auf mittlerer Hitze weiterkochen. Den abgesetzten weißen Schaum an der Oberfläche abnehmen. Anschließend die halbe Zwiebel, Zimt und Kardamom sowie 1 EL Öl hinzugeben und das Fleisch fertigkochen.
- In der Zwischenzeit den Reis 15 – 20 min kochen lassen sowie die Kartoffeln und Auberginen in ausreichend Öl frittieren. Die Scheiben mit Küchenpapier trocken tupfen und warmhalten. Das fertig gekochte Hühnerfleisch vom Kochwasser entfernen, dieses aber gut mit Salz und Pfeffer würzen und aufbewahren.
- Für die Schichten den Boden eines großen Topfes mit einer dünnen Schicht Reis bedecken. Vorsichtig mit einer Lage frittierter Auberginenscheiben sowie einer Schicht frittierter Kartoffelscheiben beschichten. Anschließend mit einer Lage des restlichen Reises beschichten und diese gleichmäßig verteilen. Die Hühnerbrühe vorsichtig in die Beschichtung gießen, bis es den Reis 3 cm übersteigt und anschließend alles für 1 h bei sehr schwacher Hitze kochen lassen.
- In der Zwischenzeit das Hühnerfleisch vom Knochen entfernen und warmhalten. Den großen Topf auf eine Platte oder einen Teller umstürzen und vorsichtig anheben, um die Schichtung nicht zu zerstören. Vor dem Servieren das gekochte Hühnerfleisch auf der Schichtung verteilen.

- Begin by rinsing the chicken with water and then scrub it with salt and the juice of 1 lemon. Leave for 5 min, then rinse and pat dry. Simmer the chicken in a large pan on high for 15 – 20 min until it reaches boiling point, then turn down the heat to medium. Remove the white foam that floats to surface with a spoon. Add the onion, cinnamon, cardamom, and 1 tbsp olive oil and cook until the meat is done.
- Meanwhile, simmer the rice for 15 – 20 min and deep-fry the sliced potatoes and aubergines. Drain the fried vegetables on kitchen paper and cover. Remove the cooked chicken from the boiling water and leave to rest. Retain the cooking water and season with plenty of salt and pepper.
- Cover the bottom of a large pot with a thin layer of rice, then add a layer of aubergines, then a layer of potatoes, and then pour over the rest of the rice. Ensure that the rice is evenly spread before pouring over the chicken broth until it is 3 cm above the rice. Leave to cook on low for 1 h.
- Remove the chicken from the bone and keep warm. Finally, remove the pot from the heat and place a serving tray on top – then flip! Be careful to remove the pot slowly so as not to destroy the layering. Place the cooked chicken on top of the rice before serving.

45

FASOOLYE BZEIT

SYRIEN · SYRIA

500 g frische grüne Bohnen
500 g fresh green beans

Granatapfelmelasse
pomegranate molasses 204

1 gr. Zwiebel
1 large onion

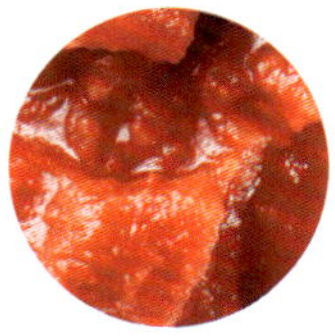

500 g Tomatenwürfel
500 g tomatoes, chopped

4 Knoblauchzehen, gehackt
4 cloves of garlic, chopped

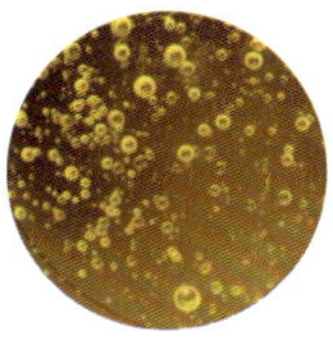

150 ml Olivenöl
150 ml olive oil

Salz, schwarzer Pfeffer
salt, black pepper

dieses Gericht ist vegan
this dish is vegan

GRÜNER BOHNENEINTOPF MIT GRANATAPFELMELASSE

GREEN BEAN STEW WITH POMEGRANATE MOLASSES

- Zuerst die Zwiebel in kleine Würfel schneiden und zusammen mit 2 EL des Olivenöls für 10 min bei mittlerer Hitze anbraten.
- Geputzte grüne Bohnen dazugeben und 15 min mit geschlossenem Deckel dünsten. Den Rest des Olivenöls sowie die Tomatenwürfel und Knoblauch hinzugeben.
- Gut verrühren und mit geschlossenem Deckel 15 min kochen lassen, bis die Tomaten glasig rot und die Bohnen saftig grün erscheinen. Gelegentlich umrühren.
- Anschließend von der Hitzequelle nehmen und für 5 min ruhen lassen. Mit Salz und Pfeffer würzen und vor dem Verzehr mit Granatapfelmelasse beträufeln.

- In a pan, heat 2 tbsp olive oil; cut the onions and fry for 10 min at medium heat.
- Then add the washed green beans and cover with the lid. Cook for 15 min. Add the chopped tomatoes, garlic, and the rest of the olive oil to the pan.
- Mix well and replace the lid, leave to cook for 15 min. Stir occasionally until the tomatoes are a bright red and the beans are a bright green.
- Remove from the heat and leave to cool for 5 min before seasoning with salt and pepper. Drizzle with molasses before serving.

FOOD BRINGS PEOPLE TOGETHER.

Noor

NOOR

Noor kommt aus Damaskus, Syrien, und wurde im Oktober dieses Jahres 24 Jahre alt. Seine große Leidenschaft ist die Fotografie sowie das Verfassen von poetischen Stücken. Er ist im März 2014 in Berlin angekommen und hat Syrien seit 2012 nicht mehr betreten. Sein begonnenes Bachelorstudium in Marketing Management in Melbourne, Australien, konnte er leider aufgrund der politischen Lage in Syrien und daraus folgender finanzieller Sorgen nicht wie geplant im September 2014 beenden.
Er reiste im Februar 2014 von Melbourne über Amsterdam zunächst nach Hamburg, um seinem kranken Cousin beizustehen. Nach drei Wochen in Hamburg wurde er in ein Wohnheim in Berlin verlegt und wartet seitdem auf seine Aufenthaltsgenehmigung. Seine weitere Zukunft ist leider ungewiss.

Linda und Faraj, Noors Kochpartner

Noor is from Damascus, Syria, and turned 24 in October 2014. He is a huge fan of photography and poetry. Noor arrived in Berlin in March 2014. The last time he set foot in Syria was in 2012 and he has not been back since. Noor travelled to Melbourne, Australia, to study for his bachelor's degree in Marketing Management, but was unable to complete his studies. He planned to have his finished degree by September 2014 but had to depart early due to financial restraints related to the political situation in Syria.
Noor travelled from Melbourne to Amsterdam with the intention of ending his journey in Hamburg, where he wanted to visit his sick cousin. After three weeks in Hamburg he was assigned to a refugee home in Berlin where he continues to await for confirmation as to whether he can stay in Germany.

Linda and Faraj, Noor's cooking partners

ESSEN BRINGT MENSCHEN ZUSAMMEN.
Noor

GALNASCH

KHOZA

45

GALNASCH

TSCHETSCHENIEN · CHECHNYA

500 g Hähnchen- oder Rindfleisch
500 g chicken or beef

1 kg Mehl
1 kg flour

1 Ei
1 egg

2 Zwiebeln
2 onions

125 g Butter
125 g butter

½ TL Salz
½ tsp salt

ICH MÖCHTE UNBEDINGT BALD MAL DIE TYPISCHE CURRYWURST ESSEN.

Khoza

TSCHETSCHENISCHE NUDELN

CHECHEN PASTA

- Das Fleisch ca. 30 min in 1 l Wasser kochen und die Brühe behalten, diese kann als Soße verwendet werden.
- Aus Mehl, Ei, Salz und ca. 500 ml Wasser einen festen Nudelteig kneten. Den Teig ausrollen und
in kleine Streifen schneiden.
- Zwiebeln in Scheiben schneiden und Butter schmelzen.
- Die Nudeln in Salzwasser 10 min kochen. Mit der Brühe, den Zwiebeln und der zerlassenen Butter servieren.

- Cook the meat for approximately 30 min in 1 l of water and retain the broth (this can be used as sauce).
- Combine flour, egg, salt, and approximately 500 ml of water to form the pasta dough.
- Chop the onions and melt the butter.
- Cook the pasta for 10 min in salted water. Serve with the broth, the onions, and the melted butter.

I WOULD DEFINITELY LIKE TO TASTE THE FAMOUS CURRYWURST SOON.

Khoza

Khoza kommt aus Tschetschenien und wohnt jetzt in einem Flüchtlingsheim in Luckenwalde in der Nähe von Berlin. Kochen hat sie sich selbst beigebracht. „Wenn ich etwas Leckeres gegessen habe, habe ich einfach gefragt, wie man es zubereitet und es dann nachgekocht“, berichtet sie.
Kochen verbindet sie dabei vor allem mit Beisammensein: „Ich denke oft an meine Eltern und daran, wie wir damals in Tschetschenien zusammen gegessen haben. Ich vermisse sie sehr. Im Flüchtlingswohnheim kochen wir aber auch oft zusammen. Ich liebe die mediterrane und die arabische Küche und habe sogar schon ein paar Wörter Arabisch gelernt!“ Schwierig ist es für sie allerdings in Luckenwalde die richtigen Zutaten, wie zum Beispiel Hal-al-Fleisch, zu bekommen.
Auch wenn sie die heimische Küche sehr mag, probiert sie gerne neue Gerichte – auch deutsche bzw. Berliner Spezialitäten. „Ich möchte unbedingt bald mal die typische Currywurst essen“, sagt sie.

Milenka und Sonja, Khozas Kochpartnerinnen

Khoza comes from Chechnya and now lives in an asylum home in Luckenwalde, not far from Berlin. She learned how to cook by herself. “Any time I ate something delicious, I always asked how to prepare it and then later tried to make it myself”, she tells.
When Khoza thinks of cooking, she thinks of togetherness. “I often think about my parents and how we ate all together in Chechnya. I miss them a lot. But people cook together in the asylum home, too. I love Mediterranean and Arabic cuisine and have already learned some words in Arabic!” But in Luckenwalde, it is sometimes difficult to find certain ingredients such as Halal meat.
Khoza is a fan of trying local cuisines and enjoys trying completely new dishes – next on the list are German and Berlin specialties. “I would definitely like to taste the famous Currywurst soon”, she tells me.

Milenka and Sonja, Khoza’s cooking partners

AMANI

FALAFEL COUSCOUS IMBATEN

60 + 24 H

FALAFEL & BABA GHANOUCH

LIBYEN · LIBYA

für die Falafel · for the falafel

330 g getrocknete Kichererbsen (nicht aus der Dose)

330 g dried chickpeas (not from the can)

1½ Zwiebeln, 1½ Knoblauchzehen

1½ onions, 1½ cloves of garlic

½ Bund frischer Koriander und frische Petersilie

½ bunch of fresh coriander and fresh parsley

½ EL Koriandersamen

½ tbsp coriander seeds

½ EL Kreuzkümmelpulver

½ tbsp cumin powder

½ grüne Paprika

½ green pepper

75 g Sesamsamen

75 g sesame seeds

½ EL Chilipulver

½ tbsp chili powder

Salz, Frittieröl

salt, frying oil

für das Baba Ghanouch · for the Baba Ghanouch

2 gr. Auberginen

2 large aubergines

1½ Zitronen

1½ lemons

1 EL Tahina

1 tbsp tahina

207

frisch geschnittene Minze, nach Belieben

fresh chopped mint, to taste

glatte Petersilie, nach Belieben

flat leaf parsley, to taste

1½ Knoblauchzehen

1½ cloves of garlic

Salz, Olivenöl Extra Vergine

salt, extra virgin olive oil

dieses Gericht ist vegan

this dish is vegan

Zubereitung der Falafel:

- Die getrockneten Kichererbsen in eine Schüssel mit ausreichend Wasser geben und diese für 24 h quellen. Die gequellten Kichererbsen abtrocknen und sicherstellen, dass sie nicht mehr feucht sind.
- Die Kichererbsen zusammen mit den gewürfelten Zwiebeln, dem Knoblauch und der Paprika in einen Mixer geben. Alle anderen Zutaten dazugeben und etwa die Hälfte der Sesamsamen aufheben. Alles mixen, bis ein kompakter Teig entsteht.
- Den Falafelteig in kleine Bällchen rollen. Die Bällchen in den restlichen Sesamsamen rollen, sodass diese die Falafel-Oberfläche bedecken.
- Reichlich Öl in einer Pfanne erhitzen. Einige der Bällchen in die Pfanne geben und frittieren, bis die Oberfläche gut gebräunt ist.
- Die Falafel nach dem Frittieren auf ein Stück Küchenpapier legen, damit dieses das überschüssige Öl absorbiert.

Zubereitung des Baba Ghanouch:

- Die Auberginen bei höchster Temperatur im Grillmodus in den Backofen legen, bis diese innen weich sind (20 – 30 min).
- Die Auberginen der Länge nach entzwei schneiden und das Fruchtfleisch mit einem Esslöffel entnehmen. Dieses mit einer Gabel zerdrücken, bis es eine homogene Masse wird.
- Dann Tahina, Salz, Zitrone, Minze, Petersilie und das Öl dazugeben und verrühren, bis alle Zutaten gut untergemischt sind. Zum Anrichten noch ein wenig frisches Olivenöl und Kräuter darübergeben.

Preparation of the falafel:

- Put the dried chickpeas in a bowl with enough water and let them soak for 24 h.
  Dry the soaked chickpeas and make sure that there is no moisture left.
- Put the chickpeas in a blender with the diced onion, garlic, and pepper. Add all the other ingredients and about half of the sesame seeds. Blend until you have a compact dough.
- Roll the falafel dough into small balls, then role the balls in the remaining sesame seeds until the entire surface is covered.
- Heat enough oil in a pan. Put the falafel balls into the pan and fry until they are well browned.
- Leave the falafel on a paper towel for a little while to absorb the oil.

Preparation of the baba ghanouch:

- Put the aubergines in the oven and grill on the highest temperature until they become soft and slushy inside (20 – 30 min).
- Cut the aubergines by the length in two parts and remove the pulp with a spoon. Then mash it with a fork until you have a homogeneous mass.
- Add tahina, salt, lemon, mint, parsley, and the olive oil. Stir it until all ingredients are well mixed in. Serve the dish in a bowl with some fresh olive oil and herbs on the top.

60

COUSCOUS

LIBYEN · LIBYA

200 g Hühnchen
200 g chicken

400 g Instant-Couscous
400 g pre-cooked couscous 203

½ grüne Paprika
½ green pepper

1 kl. Zucchini
1 small zucchini

1 Kartoffel
1 potato

1 kl. Zwiebel, 1 kl. Knoblauchzehe
1 small onion, 1 small clove of garlic

1 Karotte
1 carrot

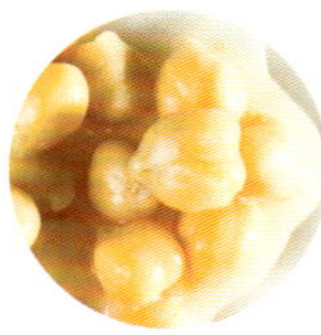

60 g Kichererbsen aus der Dose
60 g canned chickpeas

1 Tomate
1 tomato

2 Zweige Petersilie
2 sprigs of parsley

1 TL Tomatenmark
1 tsp tomato paste

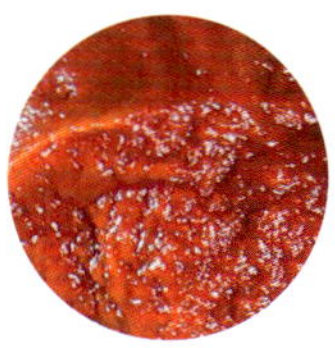

Olivenöl Extra Vergine,
Salz, Pfeffer
extra virgin olive oil, salt, pepper

COUSCOUS MIT HÜHNCHEN-GEMÜSE-SOSSE

- Das Gemüse in mittelgroße Würfel schneiden.
- Die Zwiebel und den Knoblauch schälen, beides fein hacken. Öl in einem Topf erhitzen und dann die Zwiebeln, den Knoblauch und das Hühnchen in den Topf geben. Alles anbraten, bis das Hühnchen eine leicht braune Färbung bekommt.
- Die Tomaten, das Tomatenmark und 200 ml Wasser dazugeben und alles für 15 min kochen. Das restliche Gemüse und etwas Wasser dazugeben und alles für weitere 30 – 35 min kochen, bis das Hühnchen und das Gemüse weich sind.
- Ca. 10 min bevor das Gericht fertig gekocht ist die Kichererbsen dazugeben und den Herd ausstellen. In der Zwischenzeit das Couscous nach den Instruktionen der Verpackung zubereiten.
- Das Couscous mit der Soße servieren und Petersilie darüberstreuen.

COUSCOUS WITH CHICKEN AND VEGETABLES

- Cut all vegetables into medium cubes.
- Peel and finely chop the onion and the garlic. Heat some olive oil in a pan. When the oil is hot add garlic, onions, and chicken. Roast until the meat and the onions become light brown in colour.
- Add tomatoes, tomato paste, and 200 ml water and cook for 15 min. Then add all the vegetables and more water and let it cook for 30 – 35 min until the chicken is ready and all vegetables are done.
- 10 min before the dish is done, turn off the heat and add the chickpeas.
- Meanwhile, prepare the couscous by following the instructions on the packing.
- To serve the dish, soak the couscous with the chicken-vegetables sauce and serve together with chicken and vegetables in a serving dish. At the end sprinkle some freshly cut parsley over it.

30

IMBATEN POTATOES

LIBYEN · LIBYA

1 kg Hackfleisch
1 kg minced meat

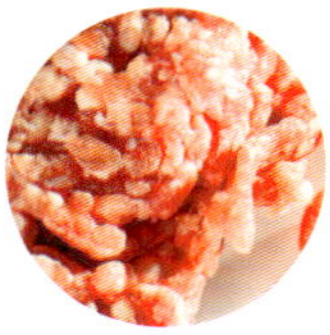

8 gr. Kartoffeln
8 large potatoes

2 Zwiebeln, 2 Knoblauchzehen
2 onions, 2 cloves of garlic

½ Bund Petersilie
½ bunch of parsley

1 TL Kreuzkümmel
1 tsp cumin

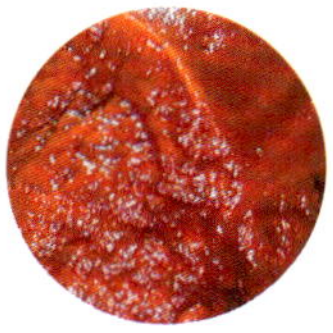

1 TL Tomatenmark
1 tsp tomato paste

3 Eier
3 eggs

Pflanzenöl zum Frittieren, Olivenöl zum Anbraten
vegetable oil for deep-frying, olive oil for frying

1 Hand voll Semmelbrösel
1 handful of breadcrumbs

Salz, schwarzer Pfeffer
salt, black pepper

statt Hackfleisch Sojafleisch verwenden
use soya meat instead of minced meat

KARTOFFEL-HACKFLEISCH-TALER

- Zwiebeln und Knoblauch schneiden und die Petersilie fein hacken.
- Das Hackfleisch mit den Zwiebeln 5 – 10 min in Olivenöl anbraten. Dann die Hitze verringern und zur Seite stellen.
- Petersilie, Knoblauch, Kreuzkümmel, Pfeffer, Salz und Tomatenmark dazugeben. Das Ganze vermischen, 1 Ei hinzugeben und gut vermengen.
- Die Kartoffeln schälen und in Scheiben schneiden.
- Ca. 1 EL der Fleischmasse zwischen 2 Kartoffelscheiben platzieren (wie ein Mini-Kartoffel-Sandwich).
- Die restlichen 2 Eier verrühren, bis eine glatte Masse entsteht und diese auf die Kartoffeln streichen.
- Danach die Kartoffeltaler in den Semmelbröseln wenden und anschließend frittieren.

POTATO AND MINCEMEAT PARCELS

- Slice the onions and garlic and finely chop the parsley.
- Fry the minced meat and onions in olive oil for 5 – 10 min, then take off the heat and leave to one side.
- Add the parsley, garlic, cumin, black pepper, salt, and tomato paste. Mix well, then crack in 1 egg and combine thoroughly.
- Peel the potatoes and cut into slices.
- Place 1 tbsp meat mixture in between 2 slices of potato (like a mini potato sandwich).
- Stir the 2 eggs until the mixture is smooth and put it on the potatoes. Then roll the potato parcels in breadcrumbs and deep-fry in vegetable oil.

AMANI

Amani kommt aus Libyen, ist 33 Jahre alt und zog erst vor zwei Monaten nach Berlin. Bevor sie nach Deutschland kam, lebte Amani vier Jahre lang in Italien, wo sie sich an den europäischen Lebensstil gewöhnte und vor allem das italienische Essen lieben lernte! Außerdem liebt sie die Natur. Trotzdem genießt sie es auch in der Stadt herumzulaufen und all die Sehenswürdigkeiten und Geräusche aufzunehmen. Wenn man mit Amani spricht, merkt man eindeutig, wie groß ihre Leidenschaft für das Kochen ist. Sie hofft eines Tages als Köchin in einem Michelin-Sternerestaurant zu arbeiten. Zusammen mit Über den Tellerrand kochen gibt sie mittlerweile Kochkurse, bei denen sie ihr Talent und ihr Wissen teilt.
Wenn man Amani nach kulturellen Gemeinsamkeiten zwischen Libyen und Deutschland fragt, antwortet sie: „Ich finde den arabischen und den europäischen Lebensstil ziemlich unterschiedlich. Aber es gibt auch einige Gemeinsamkeiten. Zum Beispiel sind Social Media Plattformen extrem wichtig für junge Menschen in Libyen – Facebook wird weitläufig genutzt und wertgeschätzt, genauso wie hier in Deutschland. Natürlich gibt es aber auch viele Unterschiede zwischen den beiden Kulturen. Ich finde das Leben in Berlin hektischer als in Tripolis, wo es, so nah am Meer, eher ruhig zugeht."

Bontu, Amanis Kochpartnerin

Amani is from Libya, 33 years old, and moved to Berlin only two months ago. Before coming to Germany, Amani was based in Italy for four years and it is there that she became well adjusted to the European lifestyle and where she developed a taste for Italian food! She loves nature but still enjoys spending time strolling around the city taking in the sights and sounds. When talking to Amani, it is clear that she has a huge passion for cooking, and she says that she one day hopes to work as a chef in a Michelin-star restaurant. Her work with Über den Tellerrand kochen extends to hosting cooking classes where she shares her talent and knowledge.
When speaking to Amani about cultural similarities between Libya and Germany she says: "I find the Arabic and European way of life to be completely different, but there are a few similarities, too. For example, social media is hugely important for the younger Libyan people – Facebook is widely used and valued, exactly the same as in Germany. There are of course differences between the two cultures, I find life in Berlin to be much more hectic than life in Tripoli, where it is quite calm near the sea."

Bontu, Amani's cooking partner

ABERAX

ZUHAIR & KAWTHER

90

ABERAX

IRAK · IRAQ

für den Eintopf · for the stew

4 Tomaten
4 tomatoes

3 Zucchini
3 zucchinis

2 – 3 kl. Auberginen
2 – 3 small aubergines

6 Kartoffeln
6 potatoes

6 Zwiebeln
6 onions

3 Knoblauchzehen
3 cloves of garlic

2 kg Mangold, nur das Grüne der Blätter verwenden
2 kg chard, only use the green part of the leaves

700 g Lammschulter, in 8 – 10 Stücken
700 g lamb shoulder, cut into 8 – 10 pieces

2 TL Baharat
2 tsp baharat
203

2 TL Salz, 2 TL Pfeffer, 1 TL Zitronensäurepulver
2 tsp salt, 2 tsp pepper, 1 tsp citric acid powder

für die Hackfleischfüllung · for the minced meat filling

200 g Hackfleisch, gebraten
200 g minced meat, fried

200 g Reis, gewaschen
200 g rice, washed

2 EL Tomatenmark
2 tbsp tomato paste

1 Knoblauchzehe, gehackt
1 clove of garlic, finely chopped

1 kl. Bund glatte Petersilie, gehackt
1 small bunch of fresh flat leaf parsley, chopped

1 TL Salz, 1 TL Pfeffer, ½ TL Zitronensäurepulver, 1 TL Baharat
1 tsp salt, 1 tsp pepper, ½ tsp citric acid powder, 1 tsp baharat

statt Lamm Seitan, statt Hackfleisch Sojafleisch verwenden
use seitan instead of lamb; soya meat instead of minced meat

Gefülltes Gemüse in einem großen Eintopf
Stuffed Vegetables in a Stew

- Tomaten aushöhlen. Zucchini und Auberginen halbieren und aushöhlen.
- Dann die Hackfleischfüllung zubereiten – dazu einfach alles mischen. Dann die ausgehöhlten Tomaten, Zucchini und Auberginen damit füllen.
- Von den Kartoffeln kleine „Deckel" abschneiden und Zucchini und Auberginen damit zudecken. Von 4 Zwiebeln die äußeren 2 Zwiebelschichten abnehmen und füllen. Die restliche Hackfleischfüllung in die Mangoldblätter einwickeln und darauflegen. In einem großen Topf die Lammschulterstücke auslegen. Darüber das gefüllte Gemüse verteilen.
- Salz, Pfeffer, Baharat und Zitronensäure zufügen, mit ca. 1 l Wasser aufkochen und 1 h bei mittlerer Hitze garen. Ab und zu Wasser nachgießen – am Ende soll keine „Brühe" im Topf sein, sondern nur ein wenig saftiger Bodensatz.
- Probieren, ob das Gemüse gar ist, den Topf vom Herd nehmen und bei geöffnetem Fenster etwas abkühlen lassen, um dann den ganzen Topf kopfüber auf eine große Platte zu stürzen. Zum Schluss die 2 restlichen Zwiebeln schneiden und in viel Öl goldbraun braten, darübergießen und verteilen.

- Hollow out the tomatoes. Cut zucchinis and aubergines in half and hollow out, too.
- For the minced meat stuffing: mix all ingredients together. Then spoon into the hollowed tomatoes, zucchini, and aubergines.
- Cut small "lids" from the potatoes and place over the filled vegetables.
- Remove the 2 outer layers of 4 onions and fill with minced meat filling, wrap the remaining minced meat stuffing into the chard leaves. Place the pieces of lamb shoulder in a large cooking pot and place all filled vegetables on top.
- Add salt, pepper, baharat, citric acid powder, and approximately 1 l of water. Cook for 1 h on medium and add water from time to time. At the end there should not be a "broth" in the pot, but only a juicy bottom.
- When the vegetables are well cooked, remove the pot from the stove and allow the stew to cool. Turn the pot upside down on a large plate. Finally, cut the remaining onion, fry with plenty of oil until they are golden brown and add to the dish.

Der 36-jährige Zuhair und die 31-jährige Kawther leben mit vier Kindern und einem Neffen seit fünf Jahren in NRW. Die Jesiden mussten den Nordirak verlassen, weil es dort keine Zukunft für sie gab.
Die Kinder gehen zur Schule, Zuhair arbeitet in einem Imbiss. Kawther hat hier Lesen und Schreiben gelernt. Die Familie ist zufrieden in Deutschland, aber die aktuelle Situation im Irak vergisst sie keinen Moment. Täglich telefoniert Zuhair mit den vom IS verfolgten Verwandten in der Heimat. Anträge auf Familienzusammenführung waren bislang erfolglos. Unterstützung kommt von der *Lohmarer Tafel*: Schon zweimal wurde gemeinsam eine große Spendenaktion für die Vertriebenen im Irak organisiert.
„Wir beten bei Sonnenaufgang und Sonnenuntergang“, erzählt Kawther nach der Mahlzeit. „Wir schließen alle Religionen in unser Gebet mit ein. Erst beten wir für die anderen. Dann auch für uns.“ Währenddessen verpackt sie große Portionen von dem köstlichen Essen – unter anderem für den alleinstehenden Nachbarn. Man sorgt für die anderen mit. Alle sind willkommen. Das durften auch wir erfahren.
Außerdem lernten wir viel über die jesidische Küche. Meist gilt es große Familien zu bekochen, gesund und frisch muss es sein. Entsprechend aufwändig sind die Rezepte. Kawther bereitet stets schon am Vortag alles vor.

Pina and Antje, Zuhairs und Kawthers Kochpartnerinnen

Zuhair, 36, and Kawther, 31, have been living with their four children and a nephew in North Rhine-Westphalia for five years now. The Yazidis had to leave Northern Iraq because there was no future for them there.
The children attend school whilst Zuhair works in a snack bar. Kawther learned to read and write in Germany. The family is satisfied with life here. However, they never forget about the situation back in Iraq. Zuhair calls his relatives daily, relatives that are being pursued by the IS. To date, all applications for family reunification have been unsuccessful. There is support from the Ecumenical project *Lohmarer Tafel*: Two fundraising projects have already been jointly organised in order to support displaced people from Iraq.
"We pray at sunrise and at sunset", Kawther says after dinner. "We include all religions in our prayers. First, we pray for others and then for us." Whilst speaking, she packs huge packages of delicious food – including packages for single neighbours. Everyone cares for everyone. Everybody is welcome. We were clearly able to see this ourselves.
We learned a lot about the Yazidi cuisine. People usually cook for large families, food that should always be fresh and healthy. Therefore, recipes can be rather complicated. Kawther usually prepares everything the day before.

Pina and Antje, Zuhair's and Kawther's cooking partners

RAFI

KABULI PALAO

90 + 1H

KABULI PALAO

AFGHANISTAN

5 gr. Tomaten
5 big tomatoes

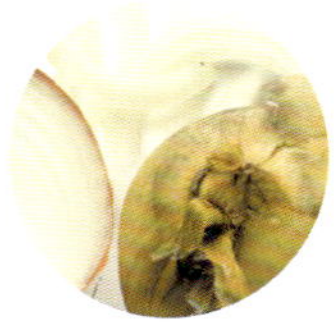

7 Zwiebeln
7 onions

6 – 7 mittelgroße Karotten
6 – 7 medium sized carrots

750 g Lammfleisch mit Knochen
750 g lamb with bones

3 Gläser afghanischer Reis oder Basmatireis
3 glasses of Afghan or basmati rice

2 – 3 Kapseln grüner Kardamom
2 – 3 green cardamom pods

204

200 g Rosinen
200 g raisins

2 frische Chilis
2 fresh chilis

Salz, Pfeffer, Pflanzenöl
salt, pepper, vegetable oil

statt Lammfleisch Tofu verwenden
use tofu instead of lamb

AFGHANISCHES REISGERICHT

AFGHAN RICE DISH

- Reis in eine Schüssel mit Wasser geben und ca. 1–2 h quellen lassen.
- Dann 2 l Wasser in einem großen Topf erhitzen.
- Zwiebeln schälen, in grobe Stücke schneiden, ins heiße Wasser geben und zum Kochen bringen. Chilis und Lamm hinzugeben. Auf hoher Stufe ca. 20 min kochen, zwischendurch umrühren.
- Eine Schüssel mit kaltem Wasser füllen und die Rosinen hineingeben, sodass sie weich werden.
- Karotten schälen, dritteln und der Länge nach schneiden. 2 EL Pflanzenöl in eine Pfanne geben und die Karotten auf hoher Stufe darin anbraten. Mit einem Deckel verschließen und einige Minuten schmoren lassen, zwischendurch umrühren. Nach ca. 10 min die Pfanne beiseitestellen, mit dem Deckel verschlossen halten.
- Die Tomaten in Stücke schneiden und zum Lamm hinzugeben. Weiterkochen lassen. Nach weiteren 10 min den Reis (mit dem Wasser), die Karotten und die Rosinen zum Lamm geben und alles 20 min unter Rühren weiterkochen.
- Grünen Kardamom hinzufügen. Den Deckel in ein Küchentuch wickeln und den Kochtopf damit bedecken. Das Küchentuch zieht Feuchtigkeit, wodurch der Eintopf gut eindickt. Bei Bedarf die Hitze reduzieren.
- Wenn der Eintopf dick eingekocht ist, den Topf vom Herd nehmen.

- Soak the rice in a bowl of water for approximately 1–2 h.
- Heat 2 l of water in a large pot.
- Peel and chop the onions, add to the hot water, and bring to boil. Add lamb and chilis. Cook on high for 20 min, stirring occasionally.
- Fill a bowl with water and add the raisins, so that they can soften.
- Peel the carrots, cut into thirds, then cut them lengthwise. Heat 2 tbsp vegetable oil and fry the carrots on high for 10 min, then set to one side with the lid on.
- Chop the tomatoes and add to the lamb. After another 10 min, add the rice (and the soaking water), carrots, and raisins. Cook for an additional 20 min, stirring occasionally.
- Add the cardamom pods. Wrap the lid in a kitchen cloth and cover the pot with it. The cloth soaks up excess liquid so that the stew thickens better. Reduce heat if necessary.
- When the stew has reached your preferred consistency, remove from the heat and serve.

RAFI

Rafi kommt aus Afghanistan und wird in diesem Jahr 19 Jahre alt. Vor etwas mehr als zwei Jahren ist er nach Düsseldorf gekommen. Im Rahmen der Jugendhilfe hat er seit einigen Monaten einen Platz in einer Wohngemeinschaft gefunden. Eine wichtige Bezugsperson ist Saaoud. Im Namen der *outback-stiftung* in Düsseldorf betreut er Rafi in dessen alltäglichen Aufgaben und unterstützt ihn dabei sich in Deutschland zurechtzufinden.
Die beiden kochen häufig und gerne zusammen.
„Das Kochen habe ich von meiner Mutter in Afghanistan gelernt. Bei uns zuhause haben wir dieses traditionelle Gericht unserer Heimat zusammen gekocht. Wenn wir bei uns Kabuli Palao essen, machen wir einen großen Topf. Dann wird ein ganzes Lamm geschlachtet und gekocht. Es ist aber auch kein Problem es alleine zuzubereiten. Ich koche sehr gern und nehme mir dann auch viel Zeit dafür. Ich finde es schön selbst zu kochen, dabei brauche ich keine Hilfe. Wenn ich dann aber koche, tue ich es am liebsten für andere. Das Essen schmeckt besser zusammen mit anderen, alleine fehlt mir der Appetit. Wenn du in ein afghanisches Restaurant gehst, bekommst du alles. Fleisch, Gemüse, Reis, Suppe. Ich selbst liebe Fleisch und am allerliebsten mag ich Lamm."

Saaoud, Rafis Kochpartner

Rafi comes from Afghanistan and will turn 19 this year. He came to Düsseldorf just over two years ago. A few months ago the youth welfare service helped him to find accommodation in a residential community. An important contact person for Rafi is Saaoud. On behalf of the *outback foundation*, Saaoud takes care of Rafi, helping him with daily tasks and supporting him to find his way in a country that he does not know very well yet. The two often cook together.
"My mother taught me how to cook back home in Afghanistan. We used to cook this traditional dish together. When we ate Kabuli Palao, we would always prepare a huge pot of it. It is a typical tradition that a whole lamb is slaughtered, prepared, and cooked for this dish – it is also not a problem to cook the dish alone! I love to cook and always take a lot of time for the preparation. However, I prefer to cook for others. It simply tastes better together and I usually have no appetite when eating alone. If you go to an Afghan restaurant, there is a huge variety: meat, vegetables, rice, soup and much more. Personally, I prefer meaty dishes – lamb in particular."

Saaoud, Rafi's cooking partner

CROM MACHSCHIE SHORBA ADS BAMIA

HANNA

60

CROM MACHSCHIE

ÄGYPTEN · EGYPT

250 g Reis
250 g rice

1 gr. Weißkohl
1 large white cabbage

2 Zwiebeln
2 onions

2 Paprikaschoten
2 peppers

2 Bund Petersilie
2 bunches of parsley

2 Bund Dill
2 bunches of dill

5 Tomaten
5 tomatoes

Butter zum Braten
butter for frying

2 Brühwürfel
2 stock cubes

Salz
salt

statt Butter Pflanzenmargarine verwenden
use vegetable margarine instead of butter

GEFÜLLTE WEIẞKOHLRÖLLCHEN
FILLED WHITE CABBAGE ROLLS

- Zwiebeln, Petersilie, Paprika und Dill klein schneiden.
- Die Tomaten mit dem Stabmixer pürieren.
- Butter in einem Topf heiß werden lassen und die Zwiebeln darin ein wenig anbraten. Anschließend die Tomatensoße dazugeben und auf kleiner Flamme köcheln lassen. Mit 1 Glas Wasser aufgießen und die Brühwürfel dazugeben.
- Das Ganze abschmecken und den Topf vom Herd nehmen. Petersilie, Dill, Paprika und Reis in den Topf hinzugeben und gut vermischen.
- Die dicken Blattstränge vom Kohl herausschneiden. Einen Topf mit viel Wasser auf dem Herd zum Kochen bringen, die Kohlblätter in das kochende Wasser geben und ca. 5 – 8 min köcheln lassen.
- Danach ca. 1 TL der Reismischung als Füllung auf ein halbes Kohlblatt geben und zusammenrollen. Wiederholen, bis die Füllung aufgebraucht ist.
- Mit den äußeren Kohlblättern einen Topf oder eine Auflaufform auslegen und die Rollen darauf platzieren.
- Anschließend den Topf mit Wasser auffüllen, sodass alle Rollen bedeckt sind. So lange leicht köcheln lassen, bis das Wasser verdampft ist (ca. 30 min). Probieren, ob die Crom Machschie gar sind, ansonsten noch einmal etwas Wasser dazugeben.

- Chop the onions and peppers into small pieces and finely chop the parsley and dill.
- Puree the tomatoes with a hand blender.
- Heat some butter in a cooking pot and fry the onions. Add the pureed tomatoes to the onions and simmer. Add 1 glass of water together with the stock cubes.
- Season the tomato mixture and take off the heat. Add the parsley, dill, peppers, and rice and mix well.
- Cut off the hard ends of the cabbage. Bring a large pot of water to boil and add the cabbage leaves. Simmer for 5 – 8 min and then strain away the water.
- Place approximately 1 tsp rice mixture onto a cabbage leaf and roll. Repeat with the rest of the mixture.
- Line a cooking pot with cabbage leaves, place the filled cabbage rolls on top and add water until all the rolls are covered. Simmer until no water is left, approximately 30 min. Test to see if the Crom Machschie is cooked, if not, add more water and simmer.

SHORBA ADS

ÄGYPTEN · EGYPT

75

2 Tassen rote Linsen
2 cups of red lentils

1 gr. Zwiebel
1 large onion

4 Knoblauchzehen
4 cloves of garlic

1 Karotte
1 carrot

1 EL Mehl
1 tbsp flour

¼ Tasse Olivenöl
¼ cup of olive oil

½ TL Kreuzkümmel
2 tsp cumin

Saft von 1 Zitrone
juice of 1 lemon

Salz, Pfeffer
salt, pepper

dieses Gericht ist vegan
this dish is vegan

ÄGYPTISCHE LINSENSUPPE

EGYPTIAN LENTIL SOUP

- Zwiebel, Knoblauch und Karotte fein hacken.
- Die Linsen zusammen mit der Karotte und der Zwiebel sowie 7 Tassen Wasser in einen großen Topf geben und ca. 1 h leicht köcheln lassen.
- Das Öl, Mehl und die Gewürze in einer Schüssel vermengen, ¼ Tasse der Suppe dazugeben und gut verrühren, sodass keine Klümpchen entstehen.
- Diese anschließend zur restlichen Suppe hinzufügen und weiter köcheln lassen, bis die Suppe schön cremig ist.
- Abschließend den Zitronensaft unter Rühren dazugeben und das Ganze etwas ziehen lassen.

- Finely chop the onion, garlic, and the carrot.
- Place the lentils, carrots, and onions into a cooking pot filled with 7 cups of water. Simmer for approximately 1 h.
- Mix together the oil, flour, cumin, salt, and pepper in a bowl. Then add ¼ of the soup to the bowl and combine well until there are no lumps left.
- Add this to the remaining soup, stir and simmer until the soup is creamy.
- Finally, add the lemon juice whilst stirring and simmer for a few more minutes.

75

BAMIA MEAT BELACHMA

ÄGYPTEN · EGYPT

206

500 g Okraschoten
500 g okras

500 g Lammfleisch
500 g lamb

2 Zwiebeln
2 onions

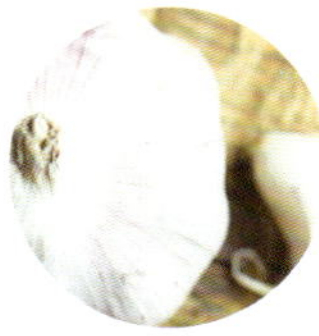

1 Knoblauchknolle
1 garlic bulb

2 EL Tomatenmark
2 tbsp tomato paste

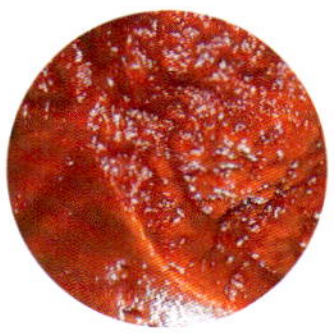

2 EL Pflanzenöl
2 tbsp olive oil

Salz, Pfeffer
salt, pepper

statt Lammfleisch Tofu verwenden
use tofu instead of lamb

Würziger Lammeintopf

Spicy Lamb Stew

- Knoblauch schälen, fein schneiden und mit Salz und Pfeffer im Mörser zerkleinern.
- Das Lammfleisch in Würfel schneiden, mit dem Knoblauchgemisch vermengen, danach 1 h gut abgedeckt im Kühlschrank ruhen lassen.
- Danach die Zwiebeln fein schneiden. Diese in erhitztem Öl zusammen mit dem Fleisch in einem großen Kochtopf gut anbraten.
- Tomatenmark in 2 Tassen Wasser auflösen, hinzugeben und bei geringer Hitze 45 min dünsten lassen, bis das Fleisch gar ist.
- Die Okraschoten in den Topf geben, vorsichtig rühren und etwa 10 min lang heiß werden lassen. Währenddessen immer wieder vorsichtig umrühren.
- Mit Salz und Pfeffer abschmecken.

- Finely chop the garlic and mince together with salt and pepper in a mortar.
- Chop the lamb into pieces, add the garlic mixture and place everything into a covered bowl. Refrigerate for 1 h.
- After the meat has rested, chop the onions and heat some oil in a pan. Fry the onions and lamb together in the pan.
- Mix the tomato paste with 2 cups of water. Add the paste to the meat and cook for approximately 45 min until the meat is done.
- Then add the okras to the meat and heat for 10 min, stirring continuously.
- Season with salt and pepper.

HANNA

Hanna ist eine unglaublich begabte Köchin. In der Küche ihrer kleinen Wohnung zaubert sie jeden Tag Köstlichkeiten, die einem das Wasser im Munde zusammenlaufen lassen. Hanna ist Ägypterin und liebt die Küche ihrer Heimat. Seitdem sie vor mehr als zwei Jahren mit ihrem Mann Farag und ihrem Sohn Dimon zunächst nach Litauen und zwei Jahre später nach Deutschland geflohen ist, nimmt das traditionelle Essen einen noch größeren Teil in ihrem Leben ein.

Als orthodoxe Christin verließ Hanna mit ihrem Mann und Sohn die geliebte Heimat, Freunde und Familie aufgrund vieler schwieriger Konflikte zwischen muslimischen und christlichen Gruppen.

In Berlin fühlt sich die kleine Familie sicher. Sogar eine eigene Wohnung haben sie schon gefunden. „Jeden Sonntag gehen wir in eine christliche Kirche, in der sowohl auf Deutsch als auch auf Arabisch gepredigt, gebetet und gesungen wird." Gerne möchte die Familie in Berlin bleiben und hier ein neues Leben anfangen. Deshalb lernt Hanna schon fleißig Deutsch aus einem kleinen Heft, das mittlerweile schon deutliche Gebrauchsspuren aufweist. So schnell wie ihr Sohn, der mittlerweile einige Sprachen fließend sprechen kann (unter anderem Deutsch), ist sie nicht. Dennoch sucht sie mutig das Gespräch, um jeden Tag ein bisschen sicherer zu werden.

Ninon, Hannas Kochpartnerin

Hanna is an incredibly talented cook. She prepares mouth-watering culinary delicacies on a daily basis in the kitchen of her small apartment. Hanna is Egyptian and adores her home country's cuisine. Along with her husband Farag and their son Dimon, Hanna fled first to Lithuania and then later to Germany. Since leaving her home country, traditional Egyptian food has become hugely significant in Hanna's life.

There are conflicts between Muslims and Christian groups in Egypt and as an orthodox Christian, Hanna was placed in a difficult position. The family had to flee and left behind not only their beloved home country, but also close relatives and friends.

Here in Berlin, the little family feels safe and they have already found a home of their own. "We go to church every Sunday – the preaching, prayers, and songs are in both German and Arabic." Hanna and her family would love to stay in Berlin to start their new life and this is why Hanna studies German every day. Her son already speaks several languages fluently, including German. Hanna courageously seeks to have as many conversations as possible in order to strengthen the language she has learned so far.

Ninon, Hanna's cooking partner

PALAT

ABDOULAYE

30

PALAT

GUINEA

1½ kg Rindfleisch ohne Knochen
1½ kg beef without bones

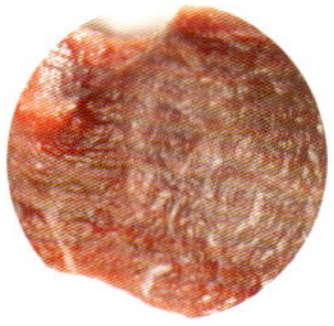

4 mittelgroße Zwiebeln
4 medium sized onions

205

3 Kochbananen
3 plantains

1 Dose rote Kidneybohnen
1 can of red kidney beans

4 Brühwürfel
4 stock cubes

1 EL Paprikapulver (edelsüß)
1 tbsp sweet paprika powder

Salz, schwarzer Pfeffer, Pflanzenöl
salt, black pepper, vegetable oil

statt Rindfleisch Seitan verwenden
use seitan instead of beef

TRADITIONELLER RINDFLEISCHEINTOPF

TRADITIONAL BEEF STEW

- Die Zwiebeln schälen und in kleine Stücke hacken.
- Die Kochbananen in Stücke schneiden und in einer Pfanne mit etwas Öl rundherum anbraten. Vom Herd nehmen und beiseitestellen.
- Das Öl in einem großen Kochtopf erhitzen.
- Die Zwiebeln in den Topf geben und bei großer Hitze kurz anbraten.
- Die Hitze reduzieren und die Zwiebeln bei geschlossenem Deckel im Öl ca. 5 min kochen, gelegentlich umrühren.
- In einem weiteren Kochtopf das Rindfleisch bei mittlerer Hitze ca. 20 min in Wasser kochen. Die Wassermenge sollte das Rindfleisch zu 3/4 bedecken. Nach 20 min schwarzen Pfeffer hinzufügen.
- Nach weiteren 10 min das Fleisch (mit dem Wasser) zu den Zwiebeln geben, umrühren und bei mittlerer Hitze weiterköcheln lassen.
- 1 EL Paprikapulver und die Brühwürfel hinzufügen und durchrühren.
- Die Hitze bei Bedarf reduzieren. Wichtig ist, dass das Ganze nur leicht köchelt.
- Nach 20 min die roten Kidneybohnen hinzufügen.
- Mit Salz abschmecken und mit den Kochbananen servieren.

- Peel the onions and chop into small pieces.
- Cut the plantains into pieces and fry in a pan with lots of oil. Once cooked, remove from the heat and set aside.
- Heat the vegetable oil in a large pot.
- Briefly fry the onions on high, then reduce heat and put on the lid. Leave to cook for approximately 5 min, stirring occasionally.
- Add the beef to another pot, pour over enough water so that ¾ of the meat is covered. Cook for 20 min, then add the black pepper, stir and leave for a further 10 min.
- Add the beef (and the cooking water) to the onions and allow to cook together.
- Add 1 tbsp paprika powder and all four of the stock cubes. Stir well.
- Allow to simmer for 20 min and then add the red beans. Stir the stew occasionally.
- Season with salt and serve with the plantains.

ABDOULAYE

Palat ist das Lieblingsessen von Abdoulayes Mutter. Zuhause kochte sie das Gericht regelmäßig und zeigte ihrem Sohn, wie man diese traditionelle Speise aus Guinea zubereitet. Ganz besonders beim Zuckerfest darf dieser leckere Eintopf nicht fehlen.
Abdoulaye ist 18 Jahre alt und kommt aus Guinea. Inzwischen ist er seit fast zwei Jahren in Deutschland. Ein Jahr wohnt er nun in einer Wohngemeinschaft, zusammen mit seinem Mitbewohner Safiullah. Sein Bezugsbetreuer Daniel und er sind seitdem ein Team. Die beiden unternehmen viel zusammen. Sie gehen joggen, schwimmen, zusammen spazieren, rudern oder Kanufahren. Ansonsten begleitet Daniel Abdoulaye bei wichtigen Amtsgängen.
Ganz besonders ist, dass Abdoulaye eine Ausbildung als Bäcker in Neuss beginnen konnte. Zuvor hatte er ein Schulpraktikum bei einer Bäckerei gemacht. Zwei Tage pro Woche war er dort, morgens um vier Uhr musste er aus den Federn. Für Abdoulaye war das kein Problem. Nach seinem Praktikum waren seine Chefs derart von seinem Einsatz begeistert, dass sie ihm einen Ausbildungsplatz anboten. Eine Ausbildung antreten zu dürfen mit einer Duldung ohne Arbeitsgenehmigung ist in Deutschland allerdings gar nicht so einfach. Drei lange Monate musste Abdoulaye hoffen und darauf warten, dass die Ausländerbehörde ihm die Genehmigung zum Antritt seiner Ausbildung gibt. Dank seines Einsatzes und dem seines Betreuers Daniel hat es dann endlich geklappt: der langersehnte Stempel auf seiner Duldung. Abdoulaye kann seinen Traum verwirklichen, er darf arbeiten.

Daniel, Abdoulayes Kochpartner

Palat is actually Abdoulaye's mother's favourite dish. She used to cook it regularly back home in Guinea and she taught Abdoulaye how to prepare the traditional stew by himself. At the end of Ramadan, during the *Eid al-Fitr* festival, this delicious stew is on offer and should not be missed.
Abdoulaye is 18 years old and was born in Guinea. He has been living in Germany for almost two years now and for one year in a shared apartment with his flat mate Safiullah. An important person in Abdoulaye's life is Daniel, his care supervisor who is on hand with help and advice anytime needed. The two of them are a real team: they spend a lot of time together. They meet to go for a walk or a jog and to swim, row or canoe together. Daniel also accompanies Abdoulaye during important appointments at governmental organisations.
Abdoulaye was able to start working full-time at a bakery in Neuss this year, having completed a training apprenticeship. Abdoulaye had to wake up at 4 am during the training period, but this was not an issue for him. His bosses were impressed by his commitment and diligence, resulting in an apprenticeship offer. However, the young man had to obtain a work permit and had to wait and hope for three months that the immigration authorities would give approval for a permanent position. It is thanks to his and Daniel's commitment that everything finally fell into place: Abdoulaye received the permit to stay and work in Germany. A dream come true!

Daniel, Abdoulaye's cooking partner

IZEE BI ISTEW

LUCAS

75

IZEE BI ISTEW

NIGERIA

300 g Hähnchenschenkel
300 g chicken drumsticks

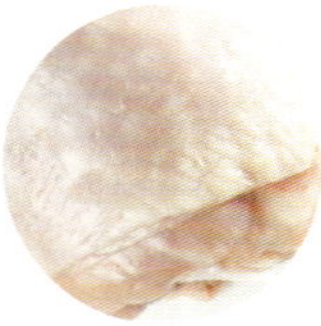

200 g Flusskrebse oder Garnelen
200 g crayfish or shrimps

2 Tassen Basmatireis
2 cups of basmati rice

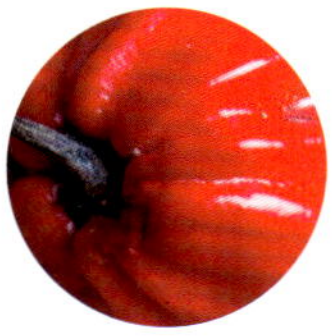

2 – 3 scharfe rote Chilis
2 – 3 spicy red chilis

6 Tomaten
6 tomatoes

2 Zwiebeln
2 onions

2 TL Currypulver
2 tsp curry powder

1 Gemüsebrühwürfel
1 vegetable stock cube

Salz, 1½ l Pflanzenöl
salt, 1½ l vegetable oil

WEIßER REIS MIT HÄHNCHEN UND GARNELENEINTOPF
WHITE RICE WITH CHICKEN AND SHRIMPS STEW

- 1 Zwiebel in grobe Würfel schneiden, Chilis grob schneiden und mit dem Hähnchenfleisch in einen Topf geben. Mit Wasser bedecken. Danach Currypulver und das Salz hinzufügen und zum Kochen bringen. Nach ca. 20 min vom Herd nehmen. Die selbstgekochte Hühnerbrühe für den Reis aufheben.
- Tomaten und die zweite Zwiebel in grobe Würfel schneiden. In einer großen Schüssel vermengen.
- 2 EL Pflanzenöl in einem Topf erhitzen. Tomaten-Zwiebel-Mischung und Salz dazugeben. Warten bis alles ein wenig eingekocht ist. Dann den Brühwürfel, ca. ¼ vom selbstgekochten Hühnerfond und die Garnelen dazugeben.
- Genug Öl in einem Topf erhitzen, um das Hähnchen zu frittieren. Die Hähnchenschenkel frittieren, bis sie goldbraun sind. Statt das Hähnchen zu frittieren, kann man es auch in den Eintopf geben und für 15 – 20 min mitkochen.
- Anschließend den Reis mit kaltem Wasser waschen, bis das Wasser klar ist und in ein Sieb geben, damit alles Wasser abfließen kann, dann in einen großen Topf schütten und mit dem Hühnerfond übergießen. Die Flüssigkeit sollte ca. 3 – 4 cm über dem Reis stehen. Wenn es nicht genügend Hühnerfond gibt, kann man den Fond mit Wasser strecken.
- Den Reis kochen, bis die Flüssigkeit verschwunden ist. Sobald der Reis fertig ist, kann er zusammen mit dem Eintopf serviert werden.

- Dice 1 onion, coarsely cut the chili in small pieces and put them together with the chicken drumsticks in a big pot. Add water until everything is covered. Then add the curry powder and the salt. Let boil for approximately 20 min. Save the chicken stock for cooking the rice.
- Dice the tomatoes and the second onion coarsely. Mix it all up in a bowl.
- Place a pot with 2 tbsp vegetable oil on the burner, pour the tomato onion mixture and salt into it. Wait until everything is a little boiled down. Then add the shrimps, the vegetable stock, and ¼ of the water you used in cooking the chicken.
- Heat a pot with enough oil to deep-fry the chicken. Fry the drumsticks until they are golden brown. If you don't want to fry, you can add the chicken to the stew and cook it there for 15 – 20 min.
- Wash the rice with cold water until the water is clean. Pour it in a sieve to drain out the water and then put it in a big pot and add the chicken stock. Make sure that the liquid is about 3 – 4 cm above the rice. If there is not enough chicken stock, add some water.
- Cook until the water is just about drying up. Check that the rice is done. When the rice is done, you can serve it with the stew.

MEIN TRAUM IST ES IN EINER GERECHTEN GESELLSCHAFT ZU LEBEN.

Lucas

MY DREAM IS TO LIVE IN A JUST SOCIETY.

Lucas

Bei unserem Besuch des morgendlichen Frühstückangebots des OESA *(Oekumenischer Seelsorgedienst für Asylsuchende)* in Basel war Lucas einer der Ersten, die uns in perfektem Englisch begrüßten. Von der Idee gemeinsam zu kochen war er sofort begeistert.
Lucas hat bereits ein Jahr in Italien gelebt. Da sich dort so gut wie keine Arbeitsmöglichkeiten für ihn ergaben, ist er nach Basel gekommen und hofft nun in der Schweiz aufgenommen zu werden. Allerdings schätzt er seine Chancen schlecht ein, da er bereits in Italien registriert wurde. Aber all das kann ihm nicht seinen Humor nehmen. Er lacht viel und erzählt begeistert von sich und davon, wie er zum Kochen gekommen ist.
Da sein Vater gestorben ist, als er noch sehr jung war, musste seine Mutter hart arbeiten, um alle sechs Kinder zu ernähren. Er erklärt, der Grund, weshalb er so gut kochen kann, ist, dass er der Jüngste der Geschwister ist. Somit ist ihm immer die Aufgabe zugefallen seine älteren Brüder zu bekochen. Sein größter Traum für die Zukunft ist es in einer gerechten Gesellschaft eine ehrliche Arbeit zu finden.

Rafael, Lucas' Kochpartner

When we first visited the breakfast meeting in Basel, which is organised every morning by the OESA *(Ecumenical Care Service for Asylum Seekers)* for the refugees of this area, Lucas was one of the first who gave us a warm welcome in perfect English. He was enthusiastic about the idea of cooking together.
When he first arrived in Europe, Lucas lived in Italy for one year. However, he could not find work there, so he decided to come to Basel. Now he hopes to get a permit to stay in Switzerland, but he does not think his chances are very good. He explains that he is already registered in Italy. But all this does not affect his happy, humorous disposition. He is laughing a lot and is enthusiastic when he tells his story and how he started with cooking.
As his father died when he was still very young, his mother had to work very hard to feed all of her six children. He says the reason why he became such a good cook is because he was the last born child and he always had to prepare the food for his older brothers. His biggest dream for the future is to have an honest work in a just society.

Rafael, Lucas' cooking partner

SAMBUSAK

SOUZAN

35

SAMBUSAK

SYRIEN · SYRIA

für den Teig · for the dough

1 kg Mehl
1 kg flour

2 TL Zucker
2 tsp sugar

1 TL Salz
1 tsp salt

4 TL Margarine
4 tsp margarine

1 Tasse warme Milch
1 cup of warm milk

1 Päckchen Trockenhefe
1 packet of dry yeast

½ Würfel Hefe in ½ Tasse warmen Wasser aufgelöst
½ yeast cube, dissolved in ½ cup of warm water

1 Ei oder etwas Milch zum Bepinseln
1 egg or milk for brushing

Schwarzkümmel oder Sesam zum Bestreuen
black caraway or sesame seeds for sprinkling

für die Spinatfüllung · for the spinach filling

1 Zwiebel, klein gehackt
1 onion, finely chopped

750 g Spinat, blanchiert
750 g spinach, blanched

bis zu ½ Tassen Granatapfelsirup, je nach Geschmack
up to ½ cup of pomegranate syrup, to taste

Pfeffer, Salz, Pflanzenöl
pepper, salt, vegetable oil

für die Rindfleischfüllung · for the beef filling

300 g Rinderhackfleisch
300 g minced beef

1 Zwiebel, gewürfelt, 1 Knoblauchzehe, zerdrückt
1 onion, chopped, 1 clove of garlic, crushed

200 g Tomatenwürfel
200 g diced tomatoes

1 TL Petersilie, fein gehackt
1 tsp parsley, finely chopped

Cayennepfeffer, Salz, Öl zum Braten
cayenne pepper, salt, oil for frying

statt Milch Sojamilch verwenden und nur die Spinatfüllung zubereiten
use soya milk instead of milk and only prepare the spinach filling

Gefüllte Teigtaschen
Filled Parcels

- Aus den Teigzutaten einen Hefeteig kneten und diesen an einem warmen Ort gehen lassen, bis die Füllung zubereitet ist.
- Für die Spinatfüllung die Zwiebeln im Öl anbraten. Anschließend den Spinat zugeben und das Ganze mit Salz, Pfeffer und Granatapfelsirup abschmecken.
- Für die Rindfleischfüllung die Zwiebel und den Knoblauch in Öl anbraten. Dann das Fleisch dazugeben und gut durchbraten. Das Ganze mit Cayennepfeffer und Salz abschmecken und zum Schluss Petersilie und Tomatenwürfel unterheben.
- Aus dem Hefeteig kleine Kugeln formen, diese mit einem Nudelholz ausrollen und mit einer Kreisform ausstechen. (Ein leeres Joghurt-Eimerchen à 1 kg eignet sich gut.)
- Mit den Füllungen bestreichen und zu Halbmonden oder Dreiecken zusammenfalten. Die Ränder dabei fest andrücken.
- Die Teile auf ein gefettetes Backblech setzen, mit Milch oder Ei bepinseln, mit Schwarzkümmel oder Sesam bestreuen und bei 180° ca. 15 min goldbraun backen.

- Place all the dough ingredients in a bowl and knead together. Put in a warm place and leave to rise whilst preparing the fillings.
- For the spinach filling: fry the onions, then add the spinach, season with salt, pepper, and pomegranate syrup.
- For the meat filling: fry the onions and the garlic in some oil, add the minced beef and fry well, season with cayenne pepper and salt, stir in the fresh parsley and the tomatoes.
- Form small balls from the dough, roll them out with a rolling pin, and cut out a circular shape. (The lid of an empty 1 kg yoghurt pot is the right size.)
- Place some filling at the centre of the dough circles and fold into crescents or triangles, press the ends firmly. Repeat with the rest of the fillings.
- Place the Sambusaks on a greased baking sheet, then brush with egg or milk, sprinkle with black caraway or sesame and then bake at 180° for 15 min until golden brown.

SOUZAN

Noch vor einem Jahr lebte Souzan in Aleppo in Syrien. Sie kam im Oktober 2013 mit ihren beiden Kindern Jad und Sama (sieben und drei) nach Ebenhausen in Unterfranken. Dort lernte sie Conny kennen, die eine Patenschaft für die kleine syrische Familie übernahm. Zusammen mit ihrer Unterstützung schaffte sie es sogar, dass Souzans Mann ihr im Juli 2014 nach Deutschland folgen konnte. Aus der Patenschaft hat sich inzwischen eine richtige Freundschaft entwickelt. Conny wurde oft zum Essen eingeladen und hat so eine richtige Begeisterung für die syrische Küche entwickelt. Jetzt sind sie gerade dabei für die Familie eine Wohnung in Ebenhausen einzurichten. Bald ziehen sie dann aus dem Asylbewerberheim in ihr neues Zuhause. Darüber freuen sie sich sehr, da sie zurzeit zu viert in einem ca. 20 bis 25 m^2 großen Zimmer wohnen müssen.
Dank der tollen Unterstützung von Conny fühlen sich Souzan und ihre Familie in Deutschland schon richtig wohl. Sie sind sehr dankbar für die Hilfe, die sie erhalten. Was sie allerdings trotzdem sehr vermisst, sind ihre guten Freunde und ihre Familie – und auch der Duft von Jasmin, der sie in ihrer Heimat umgeben hat.
Als Souzan noch in Syrien lebte, waren ihre Hobbys Fotografieren und Karate. Sie war über sieben Jahre in Folge syrische Meisterin in ihrer Gewichtsklasse und hat den schwarzen Gürtel. Darauf ist sie sehr stolz. Gerne würde sie damit auch hier in Deutschland weitermachen.

Conny, Souzans Kochpartnerin

It was just a year ago that Souzan still lived in Aleppo, Syria. In October 2013, she arrived in Ebenhausen, Unterfranken along with her children Sama, three and Jad, seven. It was in Ebenhausen that Souzan met Conny, who decided to support this Syrian family of three. Together with Conny's help, Souzan's husband was able to follow his wife to Germany in July of 2014. A true friendship has developed from what was initially only a sponsorship arrangement. Conny is often invited for dinner and has developed a real enthusiasm for the Syrian cuisine. At the moment they are arranging an apartment for the family to live in – they will soon move out of the refugee home and into a home of their own. They are very happy with this development, as they currently have to share a room that measures between 20 and 25 m^2.
Thanks to Conny's wonderful support, Souzan and her family feel at home in Germany and they are truly thankful for the help that they have received. Nevertheless, Souzan longs to see her family and close friends, she also misses the scent of jasmine that enveloped her home in Syria.
When Souzan lived in Syria, her hobbies included photography and karate. For over seven years in a row, Souzan was the Syrian champion for her weight class and is a black belt – something she is very proud of. She would love to continue karate here in Germany.

Conny, Souzan's cooking partner

KHEER

MOHAMMED

20

KHEER

PAKISTAN

100 g Milchreis
100 g rice pudding

1½ l Milch
1½ l milk

175 g Zucker
175 g sugar

25 g Kokosraspeln
25 g grated coconut

25 g Mandeln
25 g almonds

50 g Rosinen
50 g raisins

SÜßER MILCHREIS MIT ROSINEN
SWEET RICE PUDDING WITH RAISINS

- Milchreis 10 min in kaltem Wasser einweichen.
- Die Milch erhitzen.
- Rosinen zur Milch hinzufügen.
- Wenn die Milch kocht, das Wasser vom Reis abgießen und den Reis zur Milch hinzufügen.
- Unter ständigem Rühren erhitzen, bis der Brei Blasen schlägt, danach den Topf von der Herdplatte nehmen.
- Zucker unterrühren.
- Mit Kokosraspeln und Mandeln garnieren.

- Soak the rice pudding in cold water for 10 min.
- Heat the milk and then add the raisins to the milk.
- When the milk starts to boil, strain the water from the rice and add the rice to the milk.
- Stir constantly until the pudding begins to bubble.
- Remove the pan from the heat and stir in the sugar.
- Garnish with almonds and grated coconut.

MOHAMMED

Mohammed ist 16 Jahre alt. Er kommt ursprünglich aus Lahore, der zweitgrößten Stadt Pakistans. Jetzt lebt er schon seit acht Monaten mit seiner Mutter in Berlin. Demnächst wollen beide in eine kleine Zweizimmerwohnung im Zentrum der Hauptstadt ziehen. Mohammeds Mutter ist sehr krank und kann das Haus fast nie verlassen. Deshalb übernimmt Mohammed die meisten Aufgaben im Haushalt und geht auch immer alleine einkaufen. Sein größter Wunsch ist, dass seine Mutter ihm ein Geschwisterchen schenkt, um so ein wenig Unterstützung zu bekommen. Seit drei Monaten besucht Mohammed eine Schule in Berlin. Er kann sich schon sehr gut auf Deutsch unterhalten. Außerdem schreibt er gerne Gedichte in der noch relativ fremden Sprache. In Zukunft möchte Mohammed am liebsten Schauspiel studieren und ein berühmter Schauspieler werden – in Berlin natürlich, denn hier gefällt es ihm sehr gut!

Johanna, Mohammeds Kochpartnerin

Mohammed is 16 years old and originally comes from Lahore, the second largest city in Pakistan. Mohammed arrived in Berlin eight months ago along with his mother and they would both like to move into a small two-room apartment in the centre of Berlin. Mohammed's mother is very ill and can barely leave the house, therefore Mohammed holds sole responsibility for the housekeeping and must go food shopping alone. He hopes that his mum will one day have another child so that there will be another person to help out at home. Mohammed has been going to school for three months in Berlin and already speaks German to a good level, he even likes to write poems in his newly learned language! In the future Mohammed wants to study drama and become a recognised actor – in Berlin of course. He likes it here a lot!

Johanna, Mohammed's cooking partner

F&S

CHOCOLATE ALMOND CAKE

AISHE

35

CHOCOLATE ALMOND CAKE

MAZEDONIEN · MACEDONIA

für den Teig · for the batter

5 EL Zucker
5 tbsp sugar

4 Eier
4 eggs

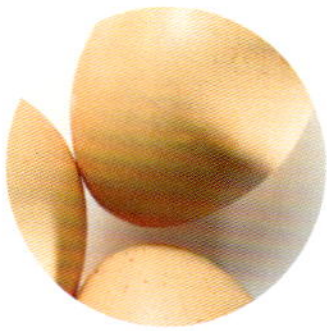

5 EL Mehl
5 tbsp flour

1 Päckchen Backpulver
1 packet baking powder

für die Schokoglasur · for the chocolate glaze

100 ml Milch
100 ml milk

4 EL Zucker
4 tbsp sugar

1 Päckchen Vanillinzucker
1 packet vanilla sugar

5 EL Kakaopulver
5 tbsp cacao powder

50 g Butter
50 g butter

für die Dekoration · for the decoration

Schokoraspeln
grated chocolate

gehackte Mandeln
chopped almonds

MAZEDONISCHER SCHOKOKUCHEN
MACEDONIAN CHOCOLATE CAKE

- Die Zutaten für den Teig in eine Rührschüssel füllen und cremig rühren.
- Eine kleine Springform fetten, leicht mit Mehl bestreuen. Den Teig einfüllen, glatt streichen und bei 200° (Ober-/Unterhitze) 25 min auf der mittleren Schiene des Backofens backen.
- In der Zwischenzeit die Zutaten für die Schokoglasur in einen Topf geben. Bei kleiner Flamme erhitzen und einige Male aufkochen lassen.
- Den Kuchen nach Ablauf der Backzeit vorsichtig aus der Form lösen und auf ein Kuchengitter legen. Die noch heiße Schokoglasur mit einem Esslöffel gleichmäßig über dem Kuchen verteilen. Den Kuchen abschließend mit Schokoraspeln und Mandeln verzieren.

Cake ist in Mazedonien ein sehr beliebter Kuchen, für den es viele Varianten gibt. Nach Belieben kann man in den Teig noch 50 g gemahlene Mandeln hineingeben. Als Verzierung eignen sich auch Kokosraspeln.

- Combine all ingredients for the cake, batter together in a bowl and mix until you have a smooth consistency.
- Grease a spring form cake tin and dust with flour. Pour the batter into the cake tin and bake at 200° (top and bottom heating) for approximately 25 min.
- In the meantime, put all the ingredients for the chocolate glaze into a small pan and heat on low. Let it boil up several times.
- Carefully remove the cake and pour the chocolate glaze evenly over the cake with a tablespoon. Decorate the cake with the grated chocolate and almonds.

Cake is a popular treat in Macedonia and exists in many varieties. For a special twist, you can add 50 g of ground almonds to the batter and for decoration, you can sprinkle over grated coconut.

ICH KOCHE MIT DEM HERZEN.
Aishe

I COOK FROM WITHIN MY HEART.
Aishe

AISHE

Nach der Trennung von ihrem Mann sah die in Skopje (Mazedonien) aufgewachsene Kosovo-Albanerin Aishe, die gebürtig aus Priština (Kosovo) stammt, in Mazedonien keine Zukunft mehr für sich und kam nach Deutschland.
Mittlerweile lebt die 33-Jährige seit fast zwei Jahren in Bochum und fühlt sich in ihrer neuen Heimat sehr wohl. Auch, weil sie hier bereits einige Freunde gefunden hat. Mit der Verständigung klappt es schon gut, aber sie möchte die Sprache möglichst schnell noch besser lernen.
Aishe träumt davon in eine kleine Wohnung umzuziehen, in der sie mehr Ruhe finden kann als im Übergangsheim. Ihr größter Traum ist aber eines Tages, wenn ihr Aufenthaltsstatus geklärt ist, ihre Tochter zu sich zu holen.

Claudia, Aishes Kochpartnerin

Aishe originates from Priština, Kosovo, but grew up in Skopje, the capital of Macedonia. After separating from her husband, Aishe could not see any future where she was and left for Germany. The 33 year old arrived in Germany nearly two years ago and settled in Bochum. She feels very comfortable in her new home country and has already made a few friends. Speaking in German works well most of the time, however Aishe wants to improve her language skills as quickly as possible. Aishe dreams about having her own little apartment where she can find more peace and quiet than in her current temporary accommodation. As soon as her residence status is confirmed, Aishe wants to bring her daughter to Germany – it would be a dream come true.

Claudia, Aishe's cooking partner

DÉGUÊ

ALI

15 + 2 H

DÉGUÊ

MALI

200 g Hirse-Couscous
200 g millet couscous

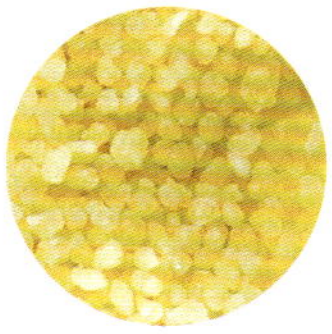

400 g Naturjoghurt
400 g natural yoghurt

300 g Vanillejoghurt
300 g vanilla yoghurt

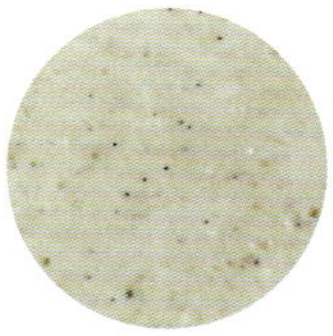

200 g gezuckerte Kondensmilch (dickflüssig)
200 g sweetened condensed milk (thick)

1 EL Butter
1 tbsp butter

100 ml Milch
100 ml milk

SÜßER HIRSE-COUSCOUS-JOGHURT
SWEET MILLET COUSCOUS WITH YOGHURT

- Hirse-Couscous mit Butter in einer großen Schüssel von Hand verrühren, bis die Körner alle voneinander getrennt sind. Nun die Masse mit aufgekochtem Wasser übergießen, bis sie vollständig abgedeckt ist. Mit einem Deckel einige Minuten stehen lassen und gelegentlich umrühren, bis das Wasser vollständig aufgenommen wurde.
- In der Zwischenzeit den Naturjoghurt mit dem Vanillejoghurt und der Kondensmilch gut verrühren.
- Die Joghurtmasse kann nun langsam in den Hirse-Couscous gerührt und vermengt werden. Danach mit 100 ml Milch übergießen. Wer Dégué noch etwas flüssiger (und süßer) mag, kann mehr Milch (und Zucker) hinzugeben.
- Vor dem Servieren mindestens 2 h im Kühlschrank kaltstellen.

- Pour the couscous and butter into a large bowl and mix together with your hands until all the grains have separated from one another. Pour boiling water over the couscous until the grains are completely covered. Put the lid on and set aside for a few minutes, stir once in a while until the water has been completely absorbed.
- Mix the natural yoghurt together with the vanilla yoghurt and the condensed milk.
- Slowly stir the yoghurt mixture into the couscous and add the milk. (If you want to have your Dégué more fluid or sweeter – simply add more milk and/or sugar.)
- Refrigerate for at least 2 h before serving.

ALI

Ich habe Ali bereits vor drei Jahren kennengelernt, als ich zur Sommeruniversität in Malta war und ausführlich damit begann mich mit dem Leben von Flüchtlingen zu beschäftigen. Ich habe die Situation hier vor Ort hautnah miterlebt und war teilweise sehr schockiert. Ali hatte zu der Zeit versucht eine Art Netzwerk von und mit anderen Migranten zu gründen, wo ich ihn bei einem Treffen kennenlernte. Sein starker Wille zu leben und zu kämpfen hat mich sehr beeindruckt.
Dieses Jahr hatte ich mich dann entschieden längerfristig nach Malta zu kommen, woraufhin ich den Kontakt mit ihm wieder persönlich aufnehmen konnte. Das heißt, wir haben uns inzwischen schon öfter getroffen, auch beieinander gegessen, doch erst jetzt bewusst zusammen gekocht. Er konnte es nicht richtig glauben, als ich ihm von der *Mach Mit!*-Aktion von Über den Tellerrand kochen erzählt habe. Wir hatten viel Spaß beim gemeinsamen Kochen und Essen.
Ali hat einen temporären Aufenthaltsstatus, der jährlich verlängert wird, ihm aber dennoch keine Sicherheit in Bezug auf Sozialleistungen bietet. Deshalb arbeitet er sehr viel, um Geld zu verdienen. Einen Teil schickt er nach Mali zu seiner Familie, den Rest muss er sparen, weil er keine Garantien hat.
Ali hat eine Tätigkeit bei einer Firma gefunden, die sich mit der Installation von Solaranlagen beschäftigt. Er möchte sich gern selbstständig machen und versucht nebenbei viele Kontakte zu akquirieren, weshalb er sehr viel unterwegs ist. Ihm gefällt es aber so. Er mag es beschäftigt zu sein. Wenn er dann doch einmal frei hat, trifft er sich gern mit Freunden.

Sabrina, Alis Kochpartnerin

I met Ali three years ago when I attended a summer school in Malta. It was during this time that I began to develop a strong interest in the lives of refugees. I witnessed the situation in Malta first-hand and was rather shocked by it. Ali took the time to build a community where refugees could meet locals and refugees alike; it is at one of these meetings that I met him. I was impressed by his strong will to live and to struggle against the odds.
This year I decided to return to Malta for a longer period and this meant that I could establish contact with Ali once again. We have been meeting regularly, spending time with each other in the kitchen and out of it. Ali could not believe it when I told him about the Über den Tellerrand kochen project! We had a lot of fun cooking and eating together .
At the moment, Ali has a temporary residence status that is renewed on an annual basis, but this offers him no security in terms of social benefits. He must work long hours in order to earn enough money to live. He sends a part of his earnings to his family in Mali and the rest he saves since he has no guarantee of future social support. Ali has found employment in a company that installs solar energy systems but he would rather be self-employed. Therefore, he is trying to acquire many new contacts – this works well as he is often on the road. If he ever has free time, he enjoys meeting friends.

Sabrina, Ali's cooking partner

DEINE EIGENEN REZEPTE UND GESCHICHTEN MACH MIT

Du hast Hunger auf mehr? Super – denn dann kannst Du Deine eigenen Kocherfahrungen und besonderen Rezepte hier notieren! Und da es in diesem Buch nicht nur um's Kochen, sondern vor allem um die Menschen geht, die Du dadurch kennenlernst, hast Du neben dem Rezept noch Platz für eine kleine Geschichte zu Deinem Kochpartner oder Deiner Kochpartnerin.

Viel Spaß beim Kennenlernen, Erleben und über den Tellerrand Kochen!

YOUR OWN RECIPES AND STORIES JOIN IN

Are you hungry for more? Great – you can write down your own cooking experiences and special recipes here! And as this book is not only about cooking, but also about the people you get to know, there is also space for a little story about your cooking partner.

Have fun getting to know new people, gathering new experiences and cooking outside of the box!

Rezepttitel · recipe name

zubereitet mit · prepared with

Zutaten · ingredients

unsere Geschichte · our story

Anleitung · instructions

Rezepttitel · recipe name

Zutaten · ingredients

Anleitung · instructions

zubereitet mit · prepared with

unsere Geschichte · our story

Rezepttitel · recipe name

zubereitet mit · prepared with

Zutaten · ingredients

unsere Geschichte · our story

Anleitung · instructions

ZUTATEN
INGREDIENTS

KENNST DU EIGENTLICH...

Rezepte aus aller Welt werden oft mit interessanten und außergewöhnlichen Zutaten zubereitet. Aber was sind eigentlich Okras? Woraus besteht Garam Masala? Und wo wachsen Johannisbrotbäume? Damit ihr immer wisst, was sich hinter den unbekannten Köstlichkeiten verbirgt, haben wir hier ein Zutatenverzeichnis für euch zusammengestellt – zum Lernen, Staunen und Ausprobieren.

DID YOU KNOW...

Recipes from across the globe are often prepared with new and unusual ingredients. But what exactly is okra? What does garam masala consist of? And where do carob trees grow? We have prepared an index of all the ingredients so that you can inform yourself about these delicacies – so that you can learn and experiment yourself!

WHENEVER YOU MEET PEOPLE FROM DIFFERENT CULTURES, YOU COOK AND EAT TOGETHER. THAT'S THE FIRST THING YOU SHARE WITH SOMEONE WHEN YOU MEET.

Noor

WENN MAN MENSCHEN AUS ANDEREN KULTUREN KENNENLERNT, KOCHT UND ISST MAN ZUSAMMEN. DAS IST DAS ERSTE, WAS MAN TEILT.

Noor

BAHARAT

Baharat ist eine oft verwendete Gewürzmischung aus dem arabischen Raum. Sie hat keine festen Bestandteile, sondern existiert in vielen Variationen mit regionalen Unterschieden. Die Hauptbestandteile sind allerdings immer Pfeffer, Paprika, Koriander, Nelken, Kreuzkümmel, Kardamom, Muskatnuss und Zimt.

BAHARAT

Baharat is a blend of spices commonly used in Arabic countries. Due to regional variations, there are no set ingredients for the mixture but baharat usually includes pepper, paprika, coriander, cloves, cumin, cardamom, nutmeg, and cinnamon.

BOMBAY BIRYANI

Die indische Gewürzmischung wird hauptsächlich für das typische Gericht Biryani, aber auch für viele andere Fleisch-, Fisch- oder Gemüsegerichte der indischen und pakistanischen Küche verwendet. Sie besteht aus Salz, Koriander, getrockneten Pflaumen, Chili, Fenchel, getrockneter Mango, Kassie, Zuckermelone, Kurkuma, Nelken, Kardamomsamen, Knoblauch, schwarzem Pfeffer, grünem Kardamom, Muskatnuss und Muskatblüten.

BOMBAY BIRYANI

This Indian spice blend is mainly used for the traditional dish Biryani, but also for meat, fish and vegetable dishes from the Indian and Pakistani cuisines. The blend consists of salt, coriander, dried plums, chili, fennel, dried mango, cassia, cantaloupe, curcuma, cloves, cardamom seeds, garlic, black pepper, green cardamom, nutmeg, and mace.

BULGUR

Bulgur kommt ursprünglich aus der Türkei und ist grober, vorgekochter Hartweizen. Er ist reisähnlich und wird größtenteils auch wie dieser gekocht und verwendet.

BULGUR

Bulgur originates from Turkey and is a coarse, pre-cooked durum wheat. It is similar to rice, and is mostly cooked and used as such.

COUSCOUS

Couscous ist ein Gericht, das hauptsächlich in der nordafrikanischen Küche vorkommt. Hergestellt wird es aus befeuchtetem und zu Kügelchen zerriebenem Hartweizengrieß, Gerste oder Hirse. Man bekommt es im türkischen Supermarkt, aber auch im Afro- und Asiasupermarkt.

COUSCOUS

Couscous is a dish that is commonly found in North African cuisine. It is made of moistened semolina, barley or millet that is then rolled into tiny balls. You can find couscous in Turkish, Afro, and Asian supermarkets.

FUFU

Fufu ist eine Art fester Brei aus Yams oder Maniok und Wasser. Alternativ kann es auch mit Mehl hergestellt werden. Er wird in Westafrika als Beilage zu vielen Speisen gereicht. Die Soße oder der Eintopf werden dann mit einem Stück Fufu mit der Hand aufgenommen. Ein großer Vorteil von Fufu ist, dass es einfach und günstig herzustellen und dennoch sehr sättigend ist. Andere Bezeichnungen sind auch Banku, Tô oder Pounded Yam.

FUFU

Fufu is a sticky mixture made from yam or cassava flour, and water – it is served as a side dish in West Africa. Sauces and stews can be eaten by hand when using a piece of Fufu to soak it up. A big advantage of Fufu is that it is easy and affordable to produce, and is also very filling. Other names for Fufu include Banku, Tô, or Pounded Yam.

GARAM MASALA

Garam Masala ist eine Gewürzmischung aus Indien. Die Hauptbestandteile sind schwarzer Kardamom, Zimt, Gewürznelken, schwarzer Pfeffer und Kreuzkümmel. Die Gewürze werden meistens gemahlen, sie können aber auch unzerkleinert gemischt werden.

GARAM MASALA

Garam masala is a blend of spices from India. The main ingredients are black cardamom, cinnamon, cloves, black pepper, and cumin. The spices are usually ground, but you can also mix them together unground.

GHEE

Ghee ist ein spezieller Butterschmalz, der aus ungesalzener Butter gewonnen wird. In Indien und Pakistan wird Ghee sehr häufig verwendet und gilt als Lebenselixier. Ghee eignet sich gut zum Braten und Frittieren und soll die Verdauung fördern, den Appetit anregen und den Körper entgiften.

GHEE

Ghee is a special clarified butter made from unsalted butter. Ghee is often used in India and Pakistan and is considered to have medicinal properties. Ghee is suitable for frying and is believed to promote digestion, stimulate appetite, and detoxify the body.

GRANATAPFELMELASSE

Granatapfelmelasse ist ein dickflüssiger Sirup, der oft in der orientalischen Küche verwendet wird oder als Zutat, um Getränke zuzubereiten. Granatapfelmelasse ist der durch Kochen reduzierte Saft aus Granatäpfeln. Die Melasse kann entweder selbst aus frischen Granatäpfeln hergestellt oder im türkischen Supermarkt gekauft werden.

POMEGRANATE MOLASSES

Pomegranate Molasses is a viscous syrup that is often used in oriental cuisine or as an ingredient when mixing drinks. Pomegranate Molasses is the reduced juice of cooked pomegranate and can either be homemade from fresh pomegranates or bought in Turkish supermarkets.

GRÜNER KARDAMOM

Grüner Kardamom gehört zu den Ingwergewächsen. Man verwendet meistens nur die Kardamomsamen, manchmal aber auch die getrockneten Kapselfrüchte. Die Frucht kommt ursprünglich aus Südindien, Irak, Thailand und Sri Lanka. In arabischen Ländern wird dem Kardamom eine aphrodisierende Wirkung nachgesagt.

GREEN CARDAMOM

Green cardamom is related to ginger. You usually cook only with the cardamom seeds, but the dried capsule is occasionally used. Cardamom stems from South India, Iraq, Thailand, and Sri Lanka. In Arabic countries it is said that cardamom is an aphrodisiac.

JOHANNISBROTBAUMSAMEN
Der Johannisbrotbaum kommt vor allem in Vorderasien und im Mittelmeerraum vor. Es ist ein immergrüner Baum mit einer Wuchshöhe von bis zu 20 m. Die Frucht des Baums ist eine dunkle, stark gebogene Hülse, in der sich Samen befinden, welche gegessen werden können. In jeder Hülse befinden sich ca. 10 – 15 Samen.

CAROB SEEDS
The carob tree grows mostly in the Middle East and areas of the Mediterranean. It is an evergreen tree that grows to heights of 20 m. The fruit of the tree is a dark, curved pod, in which you find edible seeds. In each pod there are approximately 10 – 15 seeds.

KICHERERBSENMEHL
Kichererbsenmehl besteht aus sehr klein gemahlenen Kichererbsen. Diese zählen zu den Hülsenfrüchten, mit Erbsen sind sie nicht verwandt. Man kann es im türkischen oder im Asiasupermarkt kaufen.

CHICKPEA FLOUR
Chickpea flour is made from finely ground chickpeas, which are actually classed as pulses and are not related to peas. You can buy chickpea flour in Turkish and Asian supermarkets.

KOCHBANANEN
Die aus Westafrika stammenden Kochbananen sind mit den uns bekannten Bananen verwandt, werden aber selten roh gegessen. Meistens isst man sie – ähnlich wie Kartoffeln – gekocht, gebraten oder frittiert. Wichtig ist, dass sie erst reif sind, wenn sich ihre Schale dunkel färbt. Kaufen kann man sie im Afrosupermarkt.

PLANTAINS
West African plantains are related to bananas, but are rarely eaten raw. They are eaten boiled, cooked or fried – similar to potatoes. It is important to note that plantains are not ripe until their peel has darkened. You can buy this ingredient in Afro supermarkets.

MELONENKERNE
Melonenkerne können zum Kochen verwendet werden. Dafür werden sie meistens geröstet und mit Salz verfeinert. In der Türkei und in Ägypten werden die Kerne zum Beispiel wegen ihres hohen Proteingehalts geschätzt und häufig verwendet.

MELON SEEDS
Melon seeds can be used for cooking. They are usually roasted and served with salt. In Turkey and Egypt they are valued for their high protein content and are frequently used in cooking.

OGBONO
Ogbono sind die getrockneten Kerne der afrikanischen Mango. Die Kerne haben eine nussähnliche Konsistenz und sind in Westafrika vor allem wegen ihres hohen Proteingehalts beliebt. In Deutschland findet man sie im Afrosupermarkt.

OGBONO
Ogbono is the dried seed of the African mango. The seeds of this fruit have a nutty consistency and are popular in West Africa for their high protein content. In Germany you will find them in Afro shops.

OKRA

Die aus Äthiopien stammenden Okraschoten gehören zu den ältesten Gemüsesorten der Welt. Sie sind länglich und grün und werden bis zu 20 cm groß. In den Schoten befinden sich weiße Samen, die mitgegessen werden können. Okras bekommt man im Afro- und Asiasupermarkt.

OKRA

Okras, or ladyfingers, originate from Ethiopia and are one of the oldest vegetables in the world. They are long and green and grow up to 20 cm long; they contain small white edible seeds. Okra can be bought in Afro and Asian shops.

PALMÖL

Palmöl ist ein pflanzliches Öl, das aus dem Fruchtfleisch von Ölpalmen gewonnen wird. Aufgrund seines hohen Carotingehalts hat das Öl eine orange-rötliche Farbe. Es kommt ursprünglich aus Malaysia und Indonesien, wird aber viel in der westafrikanischen Küche verwendet. Kaufen kann man es im Afro- und im Asiasupermarkt.

PALM OIL

Palm oil is a vegetable oil that is made from the pulp of oil palms. Due to the high level of carotene in the oil, it has a red-orange colour. The oil originally comes from Malaysia and Indonesia, but is now mostly used in West Africa. You can buy it in Afro and Asian shops.

PARATHA

Paratha ist ein indisches Fladenbrot. Übersetzt heißt es „Schichten aus gebackenem Teig". Paratha bestehen aus Vollkornteig und Ghee und werden auf einer speziellen runden, gewölbten Metallplatte, dem Sac, gebacken. Man kann sie aber im Asiasupermarkt auch fertig kaufen.

PARATHA

Paratha is an unleavened Indian bread. Literally translated it means "layers of baked dough". Paratha is made with wholemeal flour and ghee; it is baked on a special round, domed metal plate, the sac. You can buy Paratha ready-to-eat in Asian shops.

PUL BIBER

Pul Biber, übersetzt Blättchenpfeffer, besteht aus getrockneten und zerstoßenen milden oder scharfen Paprikas oder Chilis. Benutzt wird es meistens in der Türkei. Oft wird es auch direkt als Gewürzmischung mit etwas Salz, Pflanzenöl und Gewürzextrakten verwendet.

PUL BIBER

Translated into English as "flaked pepper", pul biber is made from dried and pounded, mild to hot paprika and chilis. It is commonly used in Turkey. It is also often used as a spice mix – along with some salt, vegetable oil, and spice extract.

SAFRAN

Safran ist eine Krokusart. Aus den getrockneten Blüten wird das gleichnamige Gewürz hergestellt. Um 1 kg zu gewinnen, benötigt man etwa 150.000 bis 200.000 Blüten aus einer Anbaufläche von ca. 10.000 m^2. Sie müssen per Hand gepflückt werden, außerdem blüht die Pflanze nur einmal jährlich. Daher zählt Safran zu den teuersten Gewürzen weltweit.

SAFFRON

Saffron is a variety of crocus. The Saffron spice is produced from the dried flowers of the Saffron plant. 150,000 to 200,000 flowers, cultivated on an area of approximately 10,000 m^2, are needed to yield 1 kg of Saffron spice. The Saffron plant blooms only once per year and the flowers must be picked by hand – this is why Saffron is one of the most expensive spices in the world.

SCHWARZAUGENBOHNEN

Die Schwarzaugenbohne kommt aus Afrika und wird dort auch viel verwendet. Schon vor 4.000 Jahren wurde sie in Westafrika angebaut. Neben den Bohnen können auch die Blätter ähnlich wie Spinat verwendet werden.

BLACK-EYED BEANS

Black-eyed beans originate from Africa and continue to be frequently used there. They were cultivated in West Africa 4,000 years ago. In addition to the beans, you can cook with its leaves as you would with spinach.

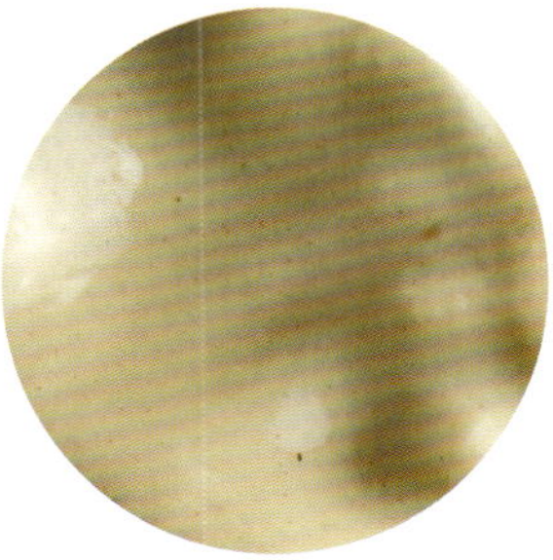

TAHINA

Tahina ist eine Paste aus fein gemahlenen Sesamkörnern. Sie stammt aus der arabischen Küche und wird vor allem für Hummus verwendet. Außerdem ist sie sehr vitaminreich und enthält viel Kalzium. Man erhält sie im türkischen Supermarkt.

TAHINA

Tahina is a paste made from finely ground sesame seeds. It originates from Arabic cuisine and is mostly used to produce hummus. It is rich in vitamins and calcium. You can buy tahina in Turkish supermarkets.

YAMS

Yams, auch Yam oder Yamswurzel genannt, ist eine hauptsächlich in den Tropen verbreitete Nutz- und Heilpflanze. Die Knollen werden bis zu 2 m lang und ähneln im Geschmack Esskastanien oder Kartoffeln, allerdings sind sie etwas süßer. Achtung: Im rohen Zustand kann die Wurzel giftig sein. Man kann sie in Afrosupermarkt kaufen.

YAM

The yam is a crop and medical plant that is widely found throughout the tropics. The bulb of the plant grows up to 2 m in length and has a similar taste to chestnuts and potatoes, but it is somewhat sweeter. Caution: The bulb may be toxic when eaten raw. You will find it in Afro shops.

YUFKA

Yufka stammt aus der Türkei. Es ist ein sehr dünner Teig aus Mehl, Wasser und Salz, der auf speziellen runden Blechen gebacken wird. Das Wort Yufka bedeutet „dünn" oder auch „zerbrechlich". In Deutschland bekommt man ihn im türkischen Supermarkt.

YUFKA

Yufka comes from Turkey. It is a very thin dough made from flour, water and salt – it is baked on special round baking sheets. The word Yufka means "thin" or "fragile". In Germany it is available in Turkish supermarkets.

83

ANHANG
APPENDIX

THE ÜBER DEN TELLERRAND KOCHEN TEAM

DAS TEAM, DAS ÜBER DEN TELLERRAND KOCHT

Am Anfang stand die Idee das abstrakte Flüchtlingsthema aus einem anderen Blickwinkel zu betrachten. Überall begegnen wir den Themen Flucht und Asyl. Doch statt nur darüber zu reden, möchte Über den Tellerrand kochen die Menschen, die hier zu uns nach Deutschland kommen, vorstellen und ihnen ein Gesicht geben. Seit einem Jahr nutzen wir deshalb das gemeinsame Kochen und Essen, um Flüchtlinge und Beheimatete zusammenzubringen und damit Begegnung auf Augenhöhe zu schaffen.
Wir sind acht Studenten und Studentinnen aus Berlin bei Über den Tellerrand kochen. Mit viel Motivation und Engagement setzen wir eigene Ideen und verschiedene Projekte mit und für Flüchtlinge und Asylsuchende um.
Ob durch ein erstes Kochbuch, die von Flüchtlingen geleiteten Kochkurse, Community-Treffen, bei denen in entspannter Atmosphäre gekocht und gemeinsame Projekte umgesetzt werden, oder durch unseren deutschlandweiten Aufruf, der schon dutzende Menschen verschiedener Kulturen beim Kochen zusammenbrachte: Wir möchten Plattformen der Begegnung schaffen, Plattformen, auf denen Fremde auf Augenhöhe zusammenkommen, zusammen kochen und Freundschaften schließen können. Das ist unser Rezept für ein besseres Wir!
Für dieses Buch verbrachten wir Tage und Nächte vor Computern, in der Küche und hinter der Kamera. Es fotografierten, kontaktierten, organisierten, vernetzten, kochten und schlemmten:

Bontu, Gerrit, Ninon, Caro,
Rafael, Lisa, Jenny und Lisa

From the outset, the idea was to consider the theme of asylum from a different angle. We encounter the subject of refugees and the topic of asylum everywhere we go, but at Über den Tellerrand kochen we wanted to take a new approach. We did not want to talk about refugees, but rather to them – to introduce them and tell their stories. For a year now, we have been bringing together residents and refugees to cook and eat together. We have been creating opportunities to get to know each other so that people can meet in an environment where they are equal and at ease.
We are eight students working at Über den Tellerrand kochen in Berlin. With a great deal of motivation and enthusiasm, we are implementing our own ideas and diverse projects with and for refugees.
Whether through our first cookbook, cooking classes led by refugees or our relaxed community meetings; whether through our community projects or through our Germany-wide call that brought together dozens of people from different cultures, we create platforms for new encounters; platforms on which the unknown can be discovered, where people can cook together and make friends. This is our recipe for a better us!
For this book, we spent long days and nights in front of computers, in the kitchen and behind the camera. Those who photographed, contacted, organised, connected, cooked and feasted include:

Bontu, Gerrit, Ninon, Caro,
Rafael, Lisa, Jenny, and Lisa

Danksagung

Am Ende dieses Buches wollen wir nur noch eins sagen – und das ist wichtig: DANKE!

Danke vor allem an alle, die unserem *Mach Mit!*-Aufruf gefolgt sind.
Danke an Helmut und Abiola, Wael und Rebekka, Daniel und Abdoulaye, Rafi und Saaoud, Safiullah und Milan, Claudia, Aishe, Eka und Aysun, Sabrina und Ali, Lena, Muhi und Hosama, Conny, Fatma, Ula und Souzan, Antje, Pina, Zuhair und Kawther, Khoza, Luiza, Annika, Tina, Milenka und Sonja, Noor und Linda, Caro und Suleman, Johanna und Mohammed und an alle weiteren Kochbegeisterten.
Überall in ganz Deutschland habt ihr über den Tellerrand gekocht und uns eure Rezepte zugeschickt. Ihr habt eure Lebensgeschichten und Kocherfahrungen mit uns geteilt. Ihr seid Teil von Über den Tellerrand kochen und Co-Autoren und -Autorinnen von diesem wundervollen Buch geworden. Ohne euch wäre all dies nie möglich gewesen!
Wir wollen uns aber auch bei vielen anderen bedanken, die uns durch ihr tatkräftiges Engagement bei der Entwicklung und Erstellung dieses Buches unterstützt haben. Insbesondere danken wir Meir, Fabian, Sarah, Chenming, dem Social Impact Lab, Hanne, Johanna, Nils, Jana, George und Katie.

Danke!
Euer Über den Tellerrand kochen-Team:
Bontu, Caro, Gerrit, Ninon, Rafael, Lisa, Jenny und Lisa

Acknowledgements

Now we have come to the end of the book but there is still one more thing we want to say – something important: THANK YOU!

Special thanks goes to everybody who took part in our *Join in!*-campaign. Thanks to Helmut and Abiola, Wael and Rebekka, Daniel and Abdoulaye, Rafi and Saaoud, Safiullah and Milan, Claudia, Aishe, Eka and Aysun, Sabrina and Ali, Lena, Muhi and Hosama, Conny, Fatma, Ula and Souzan, Antje, Pina, Zuhair and Kawther, Khoza, Luiza, Annika, Tina, Milenka and Sonja, Noor and Linda, Caro and Suleman, Johanna and Mohammed, and to all of our other cooking enthusiasts.
Everywhere in Germany you have been cooking outside of the box and have sent us your recipes. You have shared your life stories and cooking experiences with us. You have become a part of Über den Tellerrand kochen and co-authors of this wonderful book. We could not have done it without you!
We want to convey deep thanks to all of those people who have supported us with their active engagement in the development and writing of this book.
In particular, we would like to thank Meir, Fabian, Sarah, Chenming, the Social Impact Lab, Hanne, Johanna, Nils, Jana, George and Katie.

Thank you!
Your Über den Tellerrand kochen team:
Bontu, Caro, Gerrit, Ninon, Rafael, Lisa, Jenny, and Lisa

UNSERE CROWD

Wir danken außerdem allen, die mit ihrer Vorbestellung den Druck dieses Buches ermöglichten. Insbesondere danken wir:

OUR CROWD

We also thank those who pre-ordered their copies, you made the printing of this book possible. Special thanks goes to:

Ina Kwasniewski
Marvin Bruns
Elisabeth Spatzier
Judith Seggewiß
Miyoko Higuchi
Chenming Ha
Berhanu Fida
Thomas Wandt
Nora Tegeler
Jan Schröter
Swen Garling
Sigrid Strachwitz
Kathrin Schulze
Adrian Haßler
Jenny Ferguson
Ana Lichtwer

Anne Golde Arnold
Barbara Scholz
Melanie Becker
Niko Bondarenko
Gülcan Nitsch
Paula Böhler
Julia Hille
Maria Gross
Karin Schmidt
Martina Baumann
Nicole Nowakowski
Aarne Welschlau
Natali
Jakob van Eyk
Annette Kawa
Ikade

Caroline Schmidt
M.S.S. Heesch
Torsten Pörschmann
Meli Felden
Christiane Dreiling
Bettina Sander
Christian Lenz
Vera Schmidt
Bettina Wach
Steffen Lockan
Regina Görnert de Gutierrez
Tamara Siebenmorgen-Koch
Lisa Lorz
Robert Felten
Jan Otto
Bernd Janning

ROLLINS BAND
THE WEST MEMPHIS
www.WM3.org

TELLERAND

IMPRESSUM

2. Ausgabe, 2. Auflage Berlin 2015

Ninon Demuth, Bontu Guschke, Gerrit Kürschner, Carolin Strehmel
Über den Tellerrand kochen GbR
c/o Social Impact Lab Berlin
Muskauer Straße 24 · 10997 Berlin
www.ueberdentellerrandkochen.de

Auf den Wunsch einiger Mitwirkender keine Bilder ihrer Person zu verwenden wurde Rücksicht genommen. Namen wurden gegebenenfalls geändert.

Idee, Projektleitung, Text- und Bildbearbeitung
Ninon Demuth, Bontu Guschke, Gerrit Kürschner, Jennifer Sharrat, Rafael Strasser, Carolin Strehmel, Lisa Thaens, Lisa Wegst

Lektorat
Jana de Blank, Hanne Bohmhammel, Georgina Burnett, Katherine Stein

Gestaltung
GRACEFUL HASTE CD

Druck und buchbinderische Verarbeitung
Pinguin Druck GmbH
www.pinguindruck.de

Vertriebspartner
Münchner Verlagsgruppe GmbH

ISBN 978-3-95760-002-8